SuperWisdom

SuperWisdom

*Seven Vital Secrets for a
Rich and Purpose-Filled Life*

TOM RUSSELL

SuperWisdom Foundation
Payson, Arizona

Printed in the United States of America

ISBN 13: 978-0-9714526-8-8
ISBN 10 : 0-9714526-8-7

SUPERWISDOM FOUNDATION

P.O. Box 326

Payson, Arizona 85547

PHONE: (773) 353-8696

E-MAIL: *info@SuperWisdom.com*

www.SuperWisdom.com

❧ CONTENTS ❧

INTRODUCTION

Life's Most Vital Discovery

 SEVERAL PEOPLE WERE ON a walk with author and spiritual teacher Vernon Howard. While crossing a large paved parking lot, he called everyone's attention to a little flower that had broken through. He pointed out its perfect relevance to our inner task. The seed's yearning to express itself was so strong that a thick layer of concrete could not stop it.

People possess many different fears, but perhaps the largest one is unseen. It's the fear that we'll not be able to handle or contain the tremendous power of the awakened Heart. Therefore, we hold ourselves back. We live a life of reluctance. In this reduced state of energy all our problems "miraculously" appear.

Our inner difficulties are not what they appear to be. Worry, regret, fear, anger and loneliness are symptoms, not the cause. What is the *real* problem? It is a dormant Central Power Source. What is our purpose? To *awaken* this source and shatter the concrete of false beliefs and shallow thinking.

It is fascinating to discover that the location of the Central Power Source has been known for thousands of years. Throughout the Bible the power of the Heart is referenced more than 800 times. The dictionary defines Heart as: "The vital center and source of one's being, emotions, and sensibilities, the central or innermost part of a place or region." People often point to their physical heart as their spiritual heart, but ancient wisdom places this source in the region of our breath.

Different cultures have highlighted the Heart's supreme value in life and spirituality, even health and well-being. The Japanese have long referred to this domain as *Hara*. The Chinese have named it *Dan Tien*. One of the Bible's most interesting statements is in Proverbs 4:23: "Keep thy heart with all diligence; for out of it are the issues of life." Shakespeare chimes in, "Go to your bosom: Knock there, and ask your heart what it doth know." Buddha declares, "The way is not in the sky. The way is in the heart."

At the turn of the century Russell Conwell wrote a great little book that illustrates this thought entitled *Acres of Diamonds*. The book opens with a story about a wealthy man who sold his farm and journeyed to foreign lands in search of diamonds. Some time later the richest diamond mine in history was discovered, and it was found right on the land he once owned! The good news for us is this domain is still entirely our own. We can rediscover the rich life we have, in fact, never lost.

Sufi mystic Al-Ghazzali declares the glowing Heart wisdom:

The first step to self-knowledge is to know that thou art composed of an outward shape, called the body, and an inward entity called the heart, or soul. By "heart" I do not mean the piece of flesh situated in the left of our bodies, but that which uses all the other faculties as its instruments and servants. In truth it does not belong to the visible world, but to the invisible, and has come into this world as a traveler visits a foreign country for the sake of merchandise and will presently return to its native land. *It is the knowledge of this entity and its attributes which is the key to the knowledge of God.*"

FLEXIBILITY IS LIFE

In this book you'll learn how to stay energized through rotation and flexibility. You'll never stay bogged down for long, but will quickly recognize the signal to make a change to a different inner development activity. Anyone who has walked the spiritual path in earnest knows this to be a major issue. Things have a tendency to get stale if we stay with them too long. The answer is not to desert them, but to *move to something new* for awhile. Later we can cycle back with replenished reservoirs of vitality and insight.

The old Tareyton cigarette TV commercial stated, "I'd rather fight than switch." Well, in this book we learn a tremendous secret that's just the opposite: "I'd rather switch than fight!"

This book reveals four primary areas of inner development activity, referred to as The Four Gardens. They are:

· Gathering Knowledge
· Daily Life Practice
· Quiet Time
· Rest and Recreation

Cheerfulness blooms as you grow increasingly sensitive to the inner signal to make a change and work in another garden for awhile. You don't try to take something past the point where it serves its purpose. You are free of the prison of "should."

You'll discover an amazing way to apply spiritual principles in Garden # 2—your daily life. The method revolves around *The Language of Awakening*—a highly efficient form of spiritual self talk developed by author Vernon Howard. Right here, in your daily life, is where you can utilize and develop your seven secret powers of:

· Awareness
· Self-Observation
· Instant Choice
· Independence
· Forgiveness
· Efficiency
· Receptive Request

The Language of Awakening addresses a core challenge every seeker of wisdom confronts: How can I remember what I already know more often, and with greater intensity?

Wisdom seekers tend to have an idea of arriving somewhere, "enlightenment" perhaps. This *destinationest* mentality places our mind on the end and not the process. The wisdom we seek is *on the way*. It is in stirring the tea, walking to the living room or taking your next breath. It seems paradoxical, but the highest wisdom is found in the simplest acts. You'll discover in this book how to mine the lofty wealth in the simple. The rich life of your purpose-filled Heart will be yours.

This work gets to the core of things. Though we feel the purity and rightness of this restoration, we also experience the desert at times. So proceed with persistence and intelligent diligence, but be patient and gentle with yourself. Let the powers of your Heart unfold at their own natural pace. We're simply nudging them on with a friendly nod.

—TOM RUSSELL

❧ SECTION ONE ☙

EARLY MEETINGS
WITH THE WISE

MY FIRST GREAT LESSON—LEARNING TO FLY

ON A BEAUTIFUL SPRING day in the year 1975, I took my first flight as a student pilot. I arrived at Adams Airfield in Little Rock, Arkansas, full of excitement and anticipation. After checking the exterior of the plane, Wally, my instructor, had me enter first and sit in the pilot's seat. This concerned me, but I relaxed somewhat when I noticed there were two sets of controls.

Wally started the engine, clicked on a number of switches and got the plane ready to go. I was thrilled! How fascinating! I was going to get to watch him demonstrate what being a pilot was all about. The tower radioed that we were cleared for take-off. Wally moved onto the runway and lined up with the centerline, then turned and calmly said, "Tom, you're going to fly the plane."

What! Don't new students get to watch and learn on the first lesson? Don't books need to be studied first? Great fear took hold of me. But what could I say? I was there to learn how to fly; I just didn't think it would happen so soon! "All you have to do is pull back on the wheel when we reach 87 miles per hour. Don't worry, it's easy, you can do it."

Wally pushed on the throttle and the plane gained speed rapidly. At 87 mph Wally said, "Gently pull back, gently pull back." The plane gave a brief shake as it started to fly, making me even more stressful, if such a thing were possible.

For the next several minutes I struggled valiantly with that plane, giving it everything I had. Dipping and swaying, I fought our way up to 3000 feet. Then suddenly Wally said to me, "Tom, why don't you relax? The airplane was made to fly itself!"

For the first time in the flight I was aware that my hands were gripping the wheel, my jaw was tight, my diaphragm in knots. Then suddenly this awareness created a release. I let go! The tension dissolved and I took a deep breath. There was no need to fight. The plane leveled out and flew itself without my fierce grip. Yes! All I had to do was relax and cooperate and join the principles of flight.

We are nourished by powerful invisible currents that renew, teach and heal. We enter these currents when we let go of strained effort and realize the presence of Higher Intelligence. Like the airplane, life flies itself.

MEETING DR. CHAPIN

After both learning to fly and beginning a spiritual quest at 17 years old, I had the life changing experience of meeting Dr. Chester C. Chapin D.O. one year later. Dr. Chapin was a wise man, someone who really understood the deeper principles of life. A tall, vibrant fellow in his eighties with brilliant blue eyes, he possessed a deep, unforgettable voice that filled every inch of space when he spoke. I originally met Dr. Chapin for help with a back problem. After a few visits I said to him, "It seems to me that I have gotten used to the discomfort and I'm tensing muscles when I really don't need to." This opened the gate! He began talking about truthful principles, just spoonfuls at a time in the beginning. Within a short time my back was just fine, but he invited me to visit his office a couple of times a month for a "chat."

Over the next four years Dr. Chapin shared with me a library of wisdom. The meetings were brief, usually just ten or fifteen minutes. My spirit soared with something so different, so profound, so outside my usual self. I was an excited young man.

Dr. Chapin was a master of the Bible, with a vast knowledge of its contents. His comprehension went beyond the outer meaning to the spirit of the inner application. He often encouraged me to set aside my conditioning as to what the scriptures meant and discern the far deeper meaning of individual transformation. This was very helpful because I had met more than a few people in my young life who used the Bible to justify their cruelty and rigidity.

Dr. Chapin often referred to the Bible's frequent use of the word Heart. He said this is our Center, in the region of our breath. Indeed, this is the well from which Dr. Chapin spoke, practiced the healing art and lived his daily life. He said one day, "Let everything settle down into your Heart. Here everything is perfectly all right and could not possibly be otherwise." He also spoke frequently of the stubbornness of the human mind, how it scoffs at Heart wisdom, how it will do everything possible to deter a man or woman from finding and entering their Heart, and how we must persist in spite of everything.

About six months into our meetings and his remarkable expositions of the Bible, Dr. Chapin gave me a copy of Vernon Howard's book, *The Power of Your Supermind*. I read it with interest, but the simplicity of the book was too advanced for me. I kept reading, mainly because of Dr. Chapin's encouragement. During this period I gave Dr. Chapin a book by a then popular guru. He replied at our next meeting, "Yes, I read it, and in my opinion the author has not one percent of the understanding of Vernon Howard."

Dr. Chapin's great respect for Vernon Howard led me to order more of his books and tapes. It took awhile, but eventually the flame caught hold. I began to catch a glimpse of just how valuable this spiritual treasure is, how simple, how real, how direct!

One thing of interest I recall at this time was how threatened some people were because of my new outlook on life. My demeanor and the pitch and sound of my voice changed and it was not welcomed by those who had me "pegged." They didn't know what I was doing, and I'm forever grateful for a grain of sense that made me decide not to tell anyone about Dr. Chapin.

The fact is that change in you is a threat to those who have no wish for change. You remind them of what they should be doing with their lives, of what they have neglected, and they don't like to be reminded of that. For example, one relative became irritated because I moved and walked differently. This was very puzzling and difficult, but once we get a glimpse of Truth, we can't be stopped.

AUNT RUBY DISCOVERS A NEW DIRECTION

I brought my Aunt Ruby, who was elderly and used a walker, to see Dr. Chapin for a series of treatments. Dr. Chapin asked her if I could sit in. For the next several months I sat quietly to the side and observed as he treated her. She would then leave the room and Dr. Chapin and I would have our meeting. He said the medical establishment would point to all Aunt Ruby's conditions and proclaim there is no way she could get well. According to him, Aunt Ruby's main problem was "fixed thinking and crystallized beliefs." His osteopathic manipulation was only one small part of the process, he told me, and his primary purpose was to silently treat her thoughts to help her start to think in a new way.

One day I learned from a family member the name of Aunt Ruby's condition. In worldly terms it was indeed very serious. With a tone of heaviness and alarm I informed Dr. Chapin of the disease in private on the next visit. If a room ever shook, it did that day in Little Rock, Arkansas. Dr. Chapin boomed with immense power, "You're hypnotized!"

I watched with deep wonderment over the next several months as Aunt Ruby improved. She still used her walker but moved much better. Her disposition changed and her humor returned. Dr. Chapin recommended that she start reading Mr. Howard's books and she devoured one after the other. She couldn't get enough. Today, when anyone sulks in disappointment and tells me by their manner and sometimes their pathetic words, "It is too late for me. I had an opportunity earlier in life but passed it by," I think of Aunt Ruby. In spite of everything, she opened up and all her infirmities could not hold back the healing of her spirit.

GO WEST, YOUNG MAN

In 1980 I visited Boulder City, Nevada, to attend a week of Vernon Howard's classes at his New Life Foundation.

Vernon Howard

In the first class he told a vivid story about a man who was escorted by guards every day into a small isolated room. Here, over audio speakers, he was commanded to think about a stream of disconnected and random items. One day he decided he'd had enough and said to himself, "Regardless of the consequences, I withdraw my consent to allow the guards to escort me into this think tank." He stayed with that refusal and the guards fell apart with rage, but they could not harm him and they could not change his mind. The think tank collapsed, the guards dispersed and the man was free forever. Mr. Howard's story illustrates that we have the power of choice, and we do not have to consent to chaotic streams of thought and energy draining visits to unproductive areas of the mind.

Over the next six months I piloted my small plane out to Nevada often, and finally moved there to attend the classes regularly. The first class after making the move, I was handed a broom and cheerfully informed I was in charge of sweeping the floor. Quite different from "pilot in command."

The day I departed Arkansas, Dr. Chapin expressed how happy he was for me. He wanted to know everything that was going on at the school, so I began to take brief notes, mostly just jotting down key words to jog my memory later. When I got home, I immediately went to my typewriter to construct the summary for Dr. Chapin. In my own words, I typed the stories and illustrations Mr. Howard told, the key points and any spiritual exercises he assigned, also my own observations and discoveries. I kept copies and sent him the original. Thrilled with these letters, he was there with me in spirit all the way. I told Mr. Howard about Dr. Chapin as well. He nodded with understanding and smiled.

A year and a half after moving to Nevada, I received a letter from Dr. Chapin in which he said, "You must keep this up. Don't let anything stop you." Two weeks later, I received word that he had passed away. I kept on writing summaries of each class for the next ten years until Vernon Howard passed away in 1992. It was the rewriting of his ideas, in my own words, that made this project of utmost personal value.

In early 1992, I told Mr. Howard about my huge collection of notes outlining the stories, exercises and inspirations he had given in his classes over the years. He asked to see the material and I gave him 50 pages to review. The next time I saw him he suggested that a book be published. Efforts were made to begin the project, but the material needed a great deal of work; there were many things happening and the time just wasn't right.

If it had not been for Dr. Chapin, I probably would not have discovered Vernon Howard or maintained an interest in his work long enough for the flame to catch hold so early in life. Also, if it had not been for Dr. Chapin's request for my class summaries, I doubt I'd have done that either.

Dr. Chapin set my feet on the path to a rich and purpose-filled life. Wise words from his letters and writings are interspersed throughout this book, and I believe he is looking down with a smile.

VERNON HOWARD AND HIS SCHOOL

Vernon Howard was a cheerful man with a marvelous sense of humor. You knew he was the best friend your budding understanding ever had and that he truly wished the best for you. You also knew something else. You knew he was a fierce opponent of everything mechanical in you. He both encouraged your wish for inner growth and rebuked negativities, but always with a fresh new start immediately following the correction.

His school embodied old-fashioned virtues. The students were responsible and came from all walks of life—carpenters, business people, waiters, actors and handymen. All the educational items sold were reasonably priced. Physically, the school was clean and bright. Delicious and wholesome foods were served at monthly banquets and special occasions at which people visited from all over the world.

There was an atmosphere of cooperation and true friendship. Mr. Howard's high state of being and purity made all this possible.

Following my stewardship of the floor, my volunteer jobs at the school were mainly in two areas. I was the manager for the wholesale department and handled the contacts with bookstores who wished to stock Mr. Howard's books.

In later years I was also responsible for supervising the speakers bureau. Under Mr. Howard's direction, I coached speakers and helped them develop their presentation skills so they could convey content-rich messages in the classes and at guest speaking engagements. It was of great interest to Mr. Howard that all speakers practice the fundamentals of good public oratory. He was a strong proponent of clean and natural humor, storytelling and concise points, and he set a lofty standard in his own talks. Though his talks were filled with spontaneity, he said that he had a shoebox for each talk scheduled in the near future, and he constantly funneled related ideas into a given shoebox.

Vernon Howard gave me the most precious and rare of all gifts: He taught me how to know my True Self and not settle for secondhand knowledge. He had no interest in his students imitating him, for he taught that each person must make these discoveries firsthand. From all I observed and learned during many years under his instruction, I know that he wanted his work to be a living message for rare individuals who earnestly seek their higher purpose, and not a dogma cast in stone or a club to keep people in line. In making these ultimate discoveries, he encouraged everyone to lighten up and make as many mistakes as necessary, but to get off the bleachers and play the game.

SELF-RELIANCE CATCHING THE GUST

After Mr. Howard's passing in August of 1992, an entirely new level of learning presented itself. It was so much easier to be more aware when he was physically present. Now I, along with all his students, had to face the fact that the *baraka* (as it is called in the East)—the uplift—was for the most part borrowed. Where did we go from here? It was a great shock to us all, but a good one, a necessary one. Within a year of Mr. Howard's passing, everyone scattered. Some may say, "Why didn't everyone stay at the school and work together?" Such a thing isn't in accord with natural spiritual laws. Just as an old oak hits the ground and scatters the acorns, spiritual knowledge yearns to diffuse itself in new ways and places.

Today a small group of people at New Life Foundation carries on the important work of publishing and distributing Mr. Howard's material, and conducting other activities. I was part of this effort for a number of years. My present work, however, is with the SuperWisdom Foundation. We use internet, audio and video technology to reach people with these principles all over the world, in new and highly efficient ways.

It's interesting today to meet people who attended Mr. Howard's school. Some of these students I saw often for a dozen years. When I see them now, even though years have passed since we last met, we pick right up like we saw each other yesterday. This shows how connections can be made that are outside of time.

History reveals that a major challenge facing any authentic spiritual teaching is how to stay vibrant and transformative. Flexibility is crucial. The Taoist classic by Lao Tse has endured for 2500 years because it so powerfully reveals the essence of flexibility:

The Way is shaped by use,

But then the shape is lost.

Do not hold fast to shapes

But let sensation flow into the world

As a river courses down to the sea.

—*Tao Te Ching*

Truth is forever young. You can never freeze it in a pattern. It is moving, living, flowing.

This is the personal challenge of a true spiritual teaching. It doesn't let us settle down in a philosophy based on what has been said and done, even if it's the greatest collection of wisdom the world has ever seen, but insists that the principles be explored, lived and expressed *today*. Awareness is dynamic. It is Truth out of the box.

HEART HINTS

1. We enter these healing currents when we let go of strained effort and realize the presence of Higher Intelligence.

2. In your Heart is a pristine circulation of energy that expands when recognized, and as Dr. Chapin said, "Here everything is perfectly all right and could not possibly be otherwise."

3. When my "hypnotized beliefs" (as Dr. Chapin pointed out) imprisoned Aunt Ruby in regards to her condition and the world's interpretation of it, I likewise imprisoned myself.

4. The "think tank" collapses as we call the bluff on petty tyrants— the inner ones and the outer ones.

5. From Dr. Chapin: "You must keep this up. Don't let anything stop you."

6. Mr. Howard was amazingly new each moment; he did not see you as the person who made the mistake five minutes, five days or five years ago.

7. The old-fashioned virtues of cleanliness, thrift, honesty and responsibility are more important for growth than we may realize.

8. The aim of real spiritual teachings is your awakened Heart, which always expresses itself with refreshing originality.

9. Though we can borrow a drink of water from someone else who may have found his or her inner oasis, the day comes when we see with great clarity that we must drink from within, or all is in vain.

10. Awareness is Truth out of the box.

SECTION TWO

VITALITY THROUGH FLEXIBILITY

Just as an oil drilling company needs a huge variety of equipment and tools to get the wealth out of the ground, so we need an assortment of practical tools to mine the Heart's inherent wisdom.

Here is a preview of The Four Gardens:

GARDEN 1: GATHERING KNOWLEDGE
How can we get the seeds of knowledge past the intellect's filters so they reach deeper ground, germinate and grow? You'll learn highly effective ways to flourish in this beautiful garden of study and inquiry.

GARDEN 2: *THE LANGUAGE OF AWAKENING*
The most advanced field for our spiritual growth is daily life—right while we conduct all our activities, whether simple or complex. You can magically transform these experiences into opportunities for growth and insight. How? With *NowFacts.* Easy to remember, you

can use them either silently or audibly. They quickly remind you of a spiritual fact your Heart already knows.

All of the *NowFacts* are presented precisely as Vernon Howard gave them, collected over a 12-year period while I was in attendance at his classes. Their power to transform your life is real and substantial.

GARDEN 3: QUIET TIME

Trying to make the intellect quiet through direct efforts is an exercise in futility. There's a far richer way: Take a journey to your center! Delve into your Heart. Reside there in quietness and receptivity. When the Heart is quiet, the mind naturally follows. You'll learn things about this garden you've likely never seen or heard anywhere else before.

GARDEN 4: REST AND RECREATION

Though focused and intelligent effort are essential, strain wrecks everything. So don't hesitate to lay it all aside for a good game of tennis, a novel or whatever you enjoy doing for recreation. To ignore rest and recreation is to wind up in knots. Few things are more counterproductive than a stressed-out wisdom seeker obsessed with all the exercises.

This book reveals practical ways to develop your power of flexibility. It is the light touch that succeeds in this search. Nothing can ever be forced. You have an inner prompter that tells you when it is time to make a change. This is the real meaning of the "angels" referenced in the Bible. The "time to move" angel is so important because it awakens the others.

❧ GARDEN 1 ❧

GATHERING KNOWLEDGE

*How to Absorb Spiritual Knowledge
with Greater Profit and Efficiency*

WHEN ONE FIRST BEGINS his quest for the Heart, there is an outpouring of initial enthusiasm for collecting information. This is the longing of what is real within to expand and reconnect with everything that it already is on a higher level. It is indeed a breeze from the Higher World. When seen in another, this initial enthusiasm is an event of great beauty.

As we proceed with the spiritual journey, this initial enthusiasm may wane. More than a few have turned back at this point because they tried to recapture their enthusiasm with mental gymnastics.

My experience has been that the thirst for knowledge comes in cycles. It is certainly there at the beginning of the quest; however, after its first waning it returns on its own timetable. There are cycles where we feel like reading a lot, then there are times we want to do other things. If we fail to understand the principle of the Four

Gardens we can easily fall for clever guilt that says you "should" be reading more than you are.

Here are proven ways to plant the seeds of knowledge deeply. With them you can raise the profitability of your study to entirely new levels.

A. WRITE YOUR OWN *BOOK OF DEVELOPMENT*

Capture pearls of wisdom as you read, listen to audio CDs and attend talks. Make summaries of your insights and note your questions. Create drawings and art, or photography, if that is a talent. One good technique is to leave space around each journal entry so you can return again and again, gradually filling the page with new connections and insights.

Items in your journals or computer files are those that strike your emotions with exceptional clarity. For example, reviewing an entry from, say five years ago, may arouse the same emotional intensity today, perhaps even more, than it did when the entry was first made. This shows that spiritual insights are connected; they are not separated by time. Your spiritual memory exists in a dimension above the intellect.

Instead of working in a scattered and unfocused way, your book will help you dig deep and mine the gold from rich veins of experience. You'll more easily recall the many valuable lessons you've sometimes paid a high price to receive. Have the discipline to develop your book and you'll find over the years that no other reading is more profitable. It is the perfect way to inspire yourself.

PURPOSE TIP: "A man would do well to carry a pencil in his pocket, and write down the thoughts of the moment. Those that come unsought for are commonly the most valuable, and should be retained."

—*Francis Bacon*

B. CONTEMPLATE

The glider carried aloft by a tow plane has a fascinating parallel to the practice of contemplation. The tow plane can only go so high. At a certain point the lever is pulled and the glider soars away from the tow plane. It's now on its own.

Contemplation is the use of a single word, a concise sentence or perhaps a mental picture or parable. This is the tow plane. You focus in and allow the tow plane to carry you to a higher altitude. It's good to probe with questions; for example, "What is here I have yet to detect? What connections does this idea have to other ideas?" Or, "What am I afraid to see? What would disturb me?"

Then, when our contemplation has carried us as high as possible, we let go of the tow plane and transition to silence. Mr. Howard said, "Learn from books and classes, but most of all learn from silence."

Just as the winds under the glider's wings lift it higher, so does the silence of your Central Self take the original concept and turn it into wisdom.

Summary: Select a single word, sentence or illustration, and focus your attention on it for awhile, then pull the connection from the tow plane (the idea) and soar alone (in silence). Two steps: focus and release. Like the glider's tow plane, we release the source that brought us up to a certain height. Then, we *transcend* the word, concept or sentence, moving from theory to direct experience and revelation.

You may wish to keep a card or computer file of ideas you've used for contemplation. Note ideas with a special feeling for you, then retain these cards and revisit them from time to time. Keep adding new insights to your notes. This can be a bounty in the garden as we find that the seeds we planted, perhaps years ago, continue to sprout.

Here is a writing exercise that taps your power of contemplation: Pick a topic that baffles you. Write it down. Let thinking then occur naturally in your mind about the topic. Keep writing. Let your mind do what it wants to do instead of you trying to be the guide.

Contemplation can be done for extended periods when you're alone, but it is also a perfect use of time when you only have a few spare minutes.

C. READ ALOUD WHEN YOU'RE ALONE

Read enthusiastically and with conviction. Stand and let yourself gesture freely. You can even imagine that you are addressing a large audience, and that they are attentive and interested in applying the wisdom you're conveying. This imagined audience can be powerfully symbolic of your own thoughts as they receive new information and begin to change.

The highest, most powerful, teaching occurs as you discover the art of teaching yourself. This is the aim of all real teachings, to awaken the Inner Teacher. Reading valuable books aloud helps you make this shift in viewpoint like nothing else can. It will feel strange at first, especially as we practice reading with enthusiasm and clear enunciation. It also awakens our foremost fear that we will not be able to handle all the power of the awakened Heart.

Regular silent reading involves your intellectual center, while reading aloud adds your speech center. The more dimensions of yourself you involve in an activity, the greater the impact. Add your kinesthetic awareness of muscles and tension, and now there are three centers active in a single activity.

Like a jet pilot who skillfully monitors 20 things at once during a landing, as you develop, more and more of you is involved in a single activity. This is what it means to be focused. Try sometime putting your whole heart, mind and spirit, the whole of your being, into one single task. Start with ten minutes and expand from there.

D. STAY WITH THE SAME PAGES FOR AWHILE

This is a very effective way to plant deeply the seeds of knowledge. Dr. Chapin shared that he had benefited from this practice. In addition to your other reading, he said to select four or five pages from a truthful book, and read these same pages every night for a week just before going to sleep. After a week go to the next four pages.

The way to master flexibility is through simultaneously developing self-discipline and tenacity. The wise Taoist refers often to the dance of the yin and the yang, the soft and the hard. Buddhism illuminates the middle path of avoiding extremes. Water is the most flexible element on earth, and it is also the strongest; it carves canyons.

E. BE A METAPHOR HUNTER

This is wonderful fun. Be alert to daily life experiences, historical examples or experiences with nature that have a resemblance or connection to a spiritual principle. For example, you walk past a building site and hear one of the carpenters declare, "That's not done to our standards. Let's take that door out and do it right." This perks you up; it is a sudden ray of rightness that reminds you of the high standards you've set forth in your inner world.

Or, let's say you're watching a TV show about the early days of flying. You see old film footage of a contraption with a large disk on top which the motor moves rapidly up and down, as if to force the machine off the ground. This connects beautifully, you realize, with the principle: "Don't try to do with the mind what can only be done through the spirit."

As another example of being a metaphor hunter, let's say while on a hike you observe an old tree that has fallen into a stream. The tree is lodged but the flowing water gradually breaks it away and takes it downstream. You think with delight how the movement of Truth clears away old thinking that no longer serves your purpose.

Spiritual seekers tend to be far too passive, as though they can just sit back and listen or read and let the knowledge transform itself. My experience, and that of many others, is that it doesn't work that way. It requires initiative and effort, combined with a willingness to take risks and endure likely criticism. No teacher, no matter how gifted, can drink the water for you.

F. EXPRESS THE KNOWLEDGE YOU GATHER

This can include so many possibilities that are in harmony with your personality and gifts. Art, music and dance are healthy venues of creative expression. Likewise, being a good parent, cooking, building a home, running a business, even skillful, honest salesmanship are some of the many ways to express the knowledge you glean. If you can instruct others in your area of expertise, this gives you even more potential for gathering knowledge, and helps make things clearer.

If you enjoy writing and communication, why not write an article and send it away for publication? There are endless opportunities for this now on the internet. Or why not give a talk and express to the audience in vivid stories and mental pictures the experiences and insights you've gained.

Observe how crusty old habits get particularly jittery as you move more toward expression, research and involvement. These habits are not threatened by just passive reading or attending classes, but move into action and you'll come face to face with a whole new layer of "old self-objections."

PURPOSE TIP: There is Truth, and there is action. You must move into action with what you've learned, and let it take you beyond yourself.

"Old self-objections" also happen as you involve yourself in the circulation of higher ideas through appropriate venues. What doesn't want the light to circulate within you is the same thing that doesn't want it to circulate to others.

See yourself as a conduit of information, similar to a lake that stays pure by taking in fresh water on one side and releasing it on the other. This is a master key for a rich and purpose-filled life. Refuse to be a stagnant pond! Find ways to live what you learn. People stuck on the bleachers (by their own choice) tend to be critical of the players out on the field who are attempting to learn new things and daring to make mistakes.

We should also try new things, not as a distraction from inner emptiness, but as a means of forming new connections, making great finds in our parable hunts and exercising the mind. We need to expand our horizons and step out of familiar zones of competence. This includes finding ways to do much better what we may now do well. The discomfort of pushing the envelope, of trying new things, of being a beginner, is highly beneficial for spiritual growth.

G. TRANSFORM YOUR AUTOMOBILE INTO A ROLLING COSMIC UNIVERSITY

So much good information is now available on audio CD and MP3. Drive time on the less crowded open roads is a great place to absorb their treasures. Check out the free audio podcast "SuperWisdom Presents: Time Out for Truth" at www.TimeOutForTruth.com. But in all your listening, don't forget the enlightening value of a quiet drive as well.

H. ACQUIRE KNOWLEDGE THROUGH GROUP OPPORTUNITIES

A group where sincere men and women meet to delve deeply into life's great questions can be a powerful venue for collecting knowledge.

We often hesitate to participate in group activities because we sense, or know by personal experience, that groups can go terribly wrong. However, if you understand the downsides you can sidestep these issues. Let's look at three primary venues of group activity:

1. *Book discussion groups use a simple format with surprisingly good benefits.* Arrange the chairs in a comfortable circle and let the participants take turns reading. The facilitator should allow frequent pauses for contributions, but he or she should be careful that one person doesn't monopolize the comments. He will need to be aware of who has not participated, and at some point gently encourage them to do so. Select someone to summarize the discussion at the end of the meeting.

    Book discussion groups have much more value when they focus in on a particular teaching and avoid entering into comparisons of one teaching with another. In addition to a book, a CD or DVD can be used. Just sit close to the player so you can hit the pause button often for discussion. Contributions from participants that include personal experiences of applying the principles, and what was learned, are especially helpful and welcome.

2. *Classes with a speaker or speakers can be a wonderful way to learn.* Arrange the chairs in classroom or theater style, facing away from the main entrance and toward the front of the room. Speaking is truly an art and the spoken word can be transformational to the degree that the speaker applies the universal language of mental pictures, parables, metaphors and stories. A class for wisdom and spiritual growth is not a matter of just presenting the "facts." Great energy can flow through a room

as a skilled presenter unifies the group's attention in a shared experience of an unfolding mental picture.

Someone who wishes to be a speaker and communicate higher ideas of wisdom and spirituality in a classroom setting has a tremendous education ahead, and a wonderful opportunity for their own development. The communicator can study history, mythology, science and other subjects, looking for clear examples that serve as cups to hold the water of wisdom. The best mental pictures are often personal experiences. Even simple experiences, in which a lesson was learned, can be valuable material for a talk.

But of far greater importance than the technical and verbal skills is what is in the essence of the speaker. This is why even a three minute talk by someone who has really learned something has a way of reaching a deeper part of us.

You may not feel that speaking is the vehicle of expression for you, and that is just fine. It is certainly not a requirement. But those who wish to proceed in this field can check out the SuperWisdom resource at our subscription Website: Mental Pictures and the Universal Language: How to be the Best Wisdom Speaker You Can Be.

3. *Dialogue was used by Socrates and the ancient Greeks to search for truth and clarity.* Whereas a discussion group focuses on a given publication and mines its wisdom, dialogue is a format of open inquiry, questioning and probing. The attitude, "I am here to learn" is powerful. The attitude, "We are here to discover" can be even more so.

The dialogue facilitator is not there to lecture, but to introduce topics for exploration and keep the atmosphere clean and productive. He or she learns by experience the art of changing gears at just the right moment.

There is no end to worthy topics for dialogue, including new applications of familiar ideas, science meets spirituality and insights into the various meanings of a given mental picture or parable. The dialogue deepens as participants understand that the ideas they voice are not theirs to defend or promote, but a contribution that adds to the exploration. Dialogue is an open and honest search for truth, which means that our beliefs must be at least somewhat suspended in favor of questioning and probing.

PURPOSE TIP: Open every door, turn over every rock. There are no taboos. You must look into everything.

David Bohm, the quantum physicist, used this method of inquiry in profound dialogues with J. Krishnamurti. Toward the end of his life Dr. Bohm felt he was really on to something when it came to using dialogue for spiritual discovery.

Some excellent research is occurring today concerning how to create the best possible environment in which the magic of dialogue can blossom. This magic can be elusive, but the potential is most definitely there. Also, dialogue is not necessarily a structured, deliberate event. It can happen spontaneously, and with great energy, when a few friends explore the deeper questions of life in uninhibited and honest conversation.

SUMMARY

Gathering knowledge is one of life's most enjoyable endeavors. Our work is to collect all the facts we can about ourselves and inner-development. When we place this treasury of life-changing facts inside the mind, higher spiritual forces activate them. It is like the morning sun shining through a window and lighting up a basket of precious gems.

HEART HINTS

1. The aim is to plant the seeds of knowledge deeply using multiple means, such as reading, personal expression, discussion, listening to audios, contemplation and so on.

2. You have a special memory that connects all spiritual insights in a tapestry of inner light.

3. The power of group meetings is diluted when it turns into a comparison of one teaching with another; focus in and dig deep for maximum benefit.

4. As a fisherman teaches his son to fish so he can catch his own, a true book or teaching shows you *how to learn* and frees you from dependency.

5. One of the best ways to learn is to teach, but be on guard to the ego's desire to puff itself up as someone who now deserves respect.

6. The highest, most powerful instruction occurs as you awaken the Inner Teacher and discover the art of teaching yourself.

7. If you find a worthwhile group and choose to participate in its activities, always relate to people through your own direct experience, and not through the filter of opinions others may wish to give you.

8. Small groups can have more learning potential than large audiences; something is lost when the group gets too large.

9. Public speaking can be a marvelous way to face fears and grow, as well as pass along a cool drink of water from the oasis; however, it is just one means of expression and never a requirement.

10. The book you write for yourself, in which you collect clear bell principles and rich personal insights, has more long-term value than the greatest book ever written, but will you dare to find in yourself the discipline to start and maintain it?

❧ GARDEN 2 ❧

THE LANGUAGE OF AWAKENING

How to Use Daily Life to Spark Your Heart's Seven Sacred Energies

THE LANGUAGE OF AWAKENING is comprised of *NowFacts*—concise statements with a ton of truth packed inside. Unlike affirmations, *NowFacts* are designed for use while life is in motion—right in the midst of your daily life. They transform events into opportunities for insight.

PURPOSE TIP: The more difficult it is to remember
an inner-life principle, the more benefit and
energy our sudden remembering brings to us.

NowFacts are spoken either silently or audibly. When we first work with them we hear them resonating on the surface. That's fine. That's a start. But their power is magnified a thousandfold as we learn to feel our true voice in the corridors of our Heart. This is "conversation in heaven" (see Luke 17:21 and Philippians 3:20). Like the flower mentioned in the introduction that breaks through the asphalt and realizes its purpose, the energy awakened and released in your Center by *NowFacts* shatters all self-imposed limits.

HOW *NOWFACTS* ORIGINATED

All of the *NowFacts* (including the "related" *NowFacts*) are direct quotations from Vernon Howard, taught in his classes over a 12-year period. He referred to this self-instruction method as "Speech Teach." He said once, "If I had time I could write a book with 500 speech exercises in it." *The Language of Awakening* is a major step in this direction.

NowFacts give you a friendly no-nonsense jolt. They open a window for learning and cheerfulness. They reconnect you with timeless principles.

THE SEVEN ENERGIES OF YOUR AWAKENED HEART

What are the "seven vital secrets" referred to in the title of this book? They are energies. Each of the *NowFacts* you'll discover in *The Language of Awakening* has a purpose—to spark one of these seven energies:

1. AWARENESS: Your power to live in the now—the connecting

point of God/Truth/Reality—the doorway to a rich and purpose-filled life.

2. SELF-OBSERVATION: The power to detect thoughts moving
through the mind without claiming them as part of your essential self.

3. INSTANT CHOICE: Your power to instantly reclaim your
attention from negative mental movies so it flourishes in every
area of your life. Don't be like those who walk through their
days in a dull daze of preoccupation.

4. INDEPENDENCE: Your power to walk with sanity and integrity through a wobbly and compromising society, and live your
life based on the lofty standards of your awakened Heart. Compassion and empathy flow from true independence.

5. FORGIVENESS: Grudges and regrets are like huge boxes of
unnecessary cargo that overload an airplane, making safe flight
impossible. To launch the potential inside yourself, it is crucial
to toss out these worthless boxes once and for all.

6. EFFICIENCY: Release the pure energy of your Heart directly
into your thoughts, your activities and your relationships. Discover how you can instantly avoid the spilling of energy in
tension, needless concerns and fiery emotions.

7. RECEPTIVE REQUEST: When life is swirling around you,
when it is the hardest time to remember, *that* is the best moment
to ask for insight and wakefulness. *NowFact* requests take just a
second or two, but these moments can have more lasting benefit for your long-term growth than a two-week retreat.

PURPOSE TIP: *NowFacts* are sparks. Because the embers are already present, a spark in the right place is all we need.

The Language of Awakening is not like standard everyday information. It is not meant to be stored in the intellect. The words need to reach a deeper part of you. They seek to get past the intellect's filter and into fertile ground, where knowledge is transformed to wisdom.

Vital Secret #1:
AWARENESS
Unlock the Cheerfulness in the Present Moment

Has a ray of happiness ever reached you at an unexpected moment? Haven't you longed for these rays to break through more often, and with greater intensity?

The present moment can be compared to an island in the middle of the sea. It appears to be isolated but beneath the surface the island is one with the entire globe. Like the island, you appear to be separate from the whole of life; however, at a deeper level you are one with God/Truth/Reality and no storm has the power to disturb this connection.

Awareness is a secret known for countless centuries. It is like the letter that was well concealed by placing it out in the open in the center of the table. Its beautiful simplicity often causes it to be overlooked and unappreciated. For example:

The Buddha was asked, "What do you and your disciples practice?" He replied, "We sit, we walk and we eat." The questioner continued, "But sir, everyone sits, walks and eats." The Buddha told him, "When we sit, we know we are sitting. When we walk, we know we are walking. When we eat, we know we are eating."

P.D. Ouspensky, author of *In Search of the Miraculous* writes:

Trying to remember yourself is always right. Whatever you are doing, just try to realize that you are doing that. Effort to remember yourself is the chief thing, because without it nothing else has any value; it must be the basis of everything. Only in this way can you pass from the mechanical to a more conscious state.

PURPOSE TIP: Awareness flourishes when you remember what a deeper part of you already knows, and does so in all kinds of circumstances and events, both pleasurable and challenging, simple and complex.

Develop Awareness with these NowFacts:

A. I AM HERE.

These three words instantly release you from rambling thinking and return you to the pleasantness of the present moment. They can be used many times a day to teach the mind the supreme value of *now*.

Voice the words (silently or audibly) and let them remind you to notice as much about your environment as possible, including colors, the breeze, your posture, your voice, the room and the objects, the car you're driving and the passing scene. Awaken to the subtle! No other place is richer than *now*!

PURPOSE TIP: "I am here" unlocks the power to keep your mind where your body is. Your body is always in the present moment, so why not join it?

It is nothing short of amazing how much "I am here" opens you up for glimpses of your rich and purpose-filled life. There is no force or hard effort, just simple recognition. You can also use the related *NowFact*, "Now is happiness—now is intelligence—now is where I really want to be."

B. I WANT TO KNOW.

This is self-teaching at its best. I want to know when I'm walking across the room. I want to know when I'm talking to someone. I want to know when I'm watching TV. I want to know when I'm answering the phone. When you walk across the room, are you thinking of something else? When you talk to someone, are you concerned about the impression you're making instead of being aware of the other person? When watching TV, are you viewing the screen and knowing you're in the room, or do you get caught up by the action on the screen?

I observed something about Mr. Howard over the years at his classes that had a profound impact on me. Every time he lifted his glasses and put them on, he knew he was doing it. His movement had that special quality of awareness that is always recognizable. No wonder he was so cheerful!

We must resolve to be aware in spite of all the old habits that don't want us to be aware. And we must endure the bluff when familiar patterns object to our new resolve to turn off the autopilot and know what we're doing the moment we are doing it.

C. WHAT WILL HAPPEN IF I GO A LITTLE DEEPER?

When the heavenly winds of *now* break through, slow down and take notice of these special experiences. Don't be careless with them. Go deeper into their content by taking in as much as you can. Discover what happens when you go a little further and a little deeper.

We can never recreate these exhilarating experiences by seeking them directly. The way to guarantee their return is with *The Language of Awakening*. You reconnect to the present moment in which the cosmic winds have the opportunity to refresh you, each time with new intensity.

PURPOSE TIP: "The higher feeling grows by awareness. What we recognize and value increases."

—*Dr. Chapin*

D. I CAN USE ALL THINGS FOR MY INNER-DEVELOPMENT.

It's not just the grander events that create significant growth opportunities. You find advanced truths in the little things—tasting your food, turning on the light switch, lifting your cup of tea, reaching for the telephone, taking your next breath. The most elevating realizations are found in all the simple things we often experience at a low grade of awareness.

You can also find elevating realizations in unpleasant experiences. For example, we've all had the experience of loading software and it doesn't work as advertised. The frustration that presents itself is an option, not a necessity. We can use this difficult moment to deliberately choose calmness and intelligent action, in place of counterproductive stress that is entirely self-generated. In this situation the *NowFact* "I can use all things for my inner-development" is immensely practical. It reminds us to choose learning over resistance.

Like an inverted pyramid, problems draw their strength from mental meandering. Restore your awareness in the simple acts of daily life and watch this meandering fade away.

E. I DON'T HAVE TO BE INTERESTED IN WHAT WAS JUST SAID.

Here is a *NowFact* with exceptional practical power. I don't have to think about the water cooler gossip or the problems presented by the media. I don't have to accommodate people who hint or demand that I should think about what's on *their* minds.

This does not mean we do not have good manners; it's just that our awareness is awake and we're not so easily carried away. As our power of awareness expands, we're increasingly attracted to the cheerfulness and vitality of the present moment. Distractions hold less and less power to pull us away.

PURPOSE TIP: Let the truth flow through you. You will then know your future is 100 percent secure because your present is.

Q & A:

Q: Can you supply other methods to develop awareness?

A: There are so many ways! For example, when the phone rings, let it be a signal to wake up. Be aware of yourself walking to the phone and lifting the receiver. Notice any anxiety or expectation. Be alert to the tone of your voice as you say hello. Don't look for anything in that phone call to fulfill you. Let the experience remain pure. Remember that awareness is always strong, poised and intelligent, and knows what to say and how to act.

This telephone exercise can expand to all areas of your life. Just as you might start painting a building and cover only a little the first day, as you keep working the entire building eventually gets painted.

Another wonderful exercise is conscious dining. Simple as it sounds, there is far more to this than appears on the surface. Do not let your mind be carried away by daydreams that want to use the dinner to escape. Stay awake during the entire experience. Be aware as you lift your fork from the table. Taste the food. Use it as an opportunity to discover your rich and purpose-filled life.

Driving is another opportunity to develop awareness. Feel your hands on the wheel. Have interest and affection for what is happening *now*. Realize that even a routine drive you make every day provides an opportunity for a completely new experience.

Preoccupation dulls everything it touches, while awareness makes even the most familiar events sparkle. You perceive color and variety you did not see before. You hear sounds with greater clarity. You breathe more deeply, which is one of the healthiest things you can do on the everyday level. Your powers of intuition come alive. You handle things well. You're rightly decisive.

You're a better parent and a safer driver. The practical benefits of awareness are endless.

Q: As you said, "Keep your mind where your body is."

A: It is such a noble and sane way to live! J. Krishnamurti told a story about a man who came to see him about his many problems. A beautiful butterfly flew into the room and circled several times. The visitor was so self-absorbed, he never saw it.

In the absence of awareness, self-absorption runs rampant. People often want complicated and expensive answers. They refuse to see that happiness, wisdom and vitality can be as simple as the present moment.

Remember the letters WUN? They stand for *Wake Up Now*. Place these letters someplace where you will see them often. Let them be a reminder to you to drop all racing thoughts, come back to yourself and suddenly be awake.

Q: I'm somewhat confused as to how one can live in this world yet practice spirituality. There's so much to think about!

A: A spark of awareness can be present when you are doing daily work, conversing with others, making plans or enjoying recreation. Mr. Howard explains this perfectly in his book *Esoteric Mind Power:*

> Mechanical work supplies the visible rewards of food and other daily necessities. Mechanical work, whether that of a carpenter or a professor, is work done without an aim of self-awakening. Conscious work provides the invisible rewards of self-harmony and other spiritual necessities. Conscious work, whether that of a carpenter or a professor, is work performed while using it for inner dawning. You can do mechanical work without receiving payment, but you can never do conscious work without payment, though at times it may seem delayed. You can learn to do mechanical work consciously, and when succeeding, you have overcome the world.

Awareness makes you more capable in whatever task you undertake. It infuses a mother with tenderness while caring for her children. It lifts the business executive to new levels of effectiveness. The carpenter works with greater efficiency and skill. Awareness enhances a salesperson's ability to communicate. Whatever your work, these principles work wonders.

Q: It can sometimes be very difficult to be aware. Parts of us are eager to doze. Rambling thinking is familiar; awareness is unfamiliar. What do we do?

A: To reclaim the ground preoccupation has usurped will not be easy. People forget this. They begin to find the going rough as old habits object to the new direction. For example, at the start you may feel sleepy and somewhat lethargic as you're exercising muscles that have long been dormant. Just rest more often. Never try to force anything with strained effort.

Q: Do you have other awareness exercises you can recommend?

A: Walking is always energizing when accompanied by awareness. Feel the air on your face, see the colors come alive, feel your weight on your feet.

A problem deeper than unawareness, however, is a refusal to see that one is in fact unaware. We have such flattering pictures of ourselves, and our spiritual ones tend to be our most prized possessions. I remember a large public lecture Mr. Howard gave in Southern California in 1982. At the end of the talk he gave the audience an assignment to know they were walking through the doorway as they left the hall. I walked out without being aware, then, remembering that I forgot, I paused by the doorway to observe others as they departed. It was clear they did not know they were walking through the door, just as I had not. Their attention was elsewhere. I learned that day just how advanced these exercises are, in spite of how simple they appear.

Q: You remembered that you forgot! That seems to be what we're looking for.

A: Indeed it is. These awareness exercises help us see when we've drifted away from the oasis of the present moment, and this detection is a cool drink of water.

Q: How does the Heart fit in this discussion about awareness?

A: *NowFacts* voiced in the Heart activate energy. The sudden declaration "I am Here" assumes far greater power when we feel it with our entire being. Though it takes some creative work to feel the origination of *NowFacts* in your Center, with time the effort bears great fruit. We're so used to thinking of the intellect as the starting point of our speech, even though voice teachers have long proclaimed it to be in the region of the diaphragm. This is precious wisdom taught in the Bible and other ancient sources.

PURPOSE TIP: "Say these things in your Heart, from the Spirit of Reality, and you will know a thousand things more than you now do."

—*Vernon Howard*

HEART HINTS:

1. Employ the *NowFact* "I am here" and notice an abundance of new energy as it proves its value.

2. *NowFacts* condense an amazing amount of Truth into just a few words, making it easier for you to pause and apply.

3. When you activate your awareness with the *NowFact* "I want to know" you step out of preoccupation and discover the vast spiritual wealth inherent in simple activities.

4. Powerful truths are circulating around you *now*, trying to enter.

5. Remember J. Krishnamurti's lesson of the butterfly and notice the subtle things.

6. Awareness has a marvelous built-in appeal; the more you experience it the more you *want* to receive it.

7. Great insight can be found in what we label as unpleasant experiences, so wake up in traffic, wake up when standing in line, wake up when criticized, wake up when life seems to be overwhelming.

8. Daily life can be totally transformed when you discover how to do mechanical work consciously.

9. *NowFacts* gain even greater power and vitality as we grow out of being so timid with our internal speech, and let them resonate naturally and easily throughout our Being.

10. Know that when you have the *good feeling* of God/Truth/Reality coursing through you, with that feeling comes all good things, like comfort, confidence, security, support, everything.

Vital Secret #2
SELF-OBSERVATION
The Healing Beneath the Surface

What do we do about negative moods and persistent mental agitators that refuse to depart after we've dismissed them? If we try to force them out they only gain strength from our resistance. Is there another way?

Yes! Self-observation is a reliable energy for a rich and purpose-filled life. It admits a beam of light into the mind that lights up your thoughts, as a ray of sunlight through a window illuminates the floating dust particles dancing in the air.

One of the best descriptions of self-observation is given by P. D. Ouspensky in *In Search of the Miraculous*:

> Self-observation brings man to the realization of the necessity for self-change. And in observing himself, a man notices that self-observation itself brings about certain changes in his inner processes. He begins to understand that self-observation is an instrument of self-change, a means of awakening. By observing himself, he throws, as it were, a ray of light onto his inner processes that have hitherto worked in complete darkness. And under the influence of this light the processes themselves begin to change.

Release your self-observation energy with these NowFacts:

A. THERE IS _____ .

This *NowFact* places the light of self-observation directly on what is observed internally, instead of filtering it through an illusory and possessive "I" that wants to claim as its own all it sees and experiences. Simply fill in the blank with what you observe. For example, *there is worry, there is anger, there is tension.* This takes away the *reaction* to the disturbance by granting the disturbance space to linger without self-condemnation. "There is _____" is a simple statement of fact, and in this simplicity is its great power.

A related statement is, "I'm going to explore in spite of the fear." The word "explore" captures perfectly the meaning of self-observation. Our aim is insight, to uncover what's there—not to battle, suppress or resist. Exploration leads to bright new worlds, just as Columbus explored the horizon and discovered a continent.

PURPOSE TIP: The treasures of self-observation are found by witnessing without the slightest effort to modify. This energy is the relaxed and uncritical awareness of the events of the mind *as they occur.*

B. HOW DO I *REALLY* FEEL?

Without the screen of words, simply come face to face with how you actually feel this instant. If mental pain is present, don't try to cover it with positive thoughts. Don't go to the refrigerator or turn on the television or call someone. Seek insight, knowing you are perfectly safe when facing disturbances with the sincere desire to understand their underlying causes.

Let the ache be there! There's pure energy in the ache. This energy can be freed through understanding and through contact, not through resistance. There's wisdom in the ache! It has something to say. What a relief to give up the battle of the mind with itself.

"How do I *really* feel?" Notice how much more clarity and energy you have when you simply relax from all attempts to "feel good" and let yourself be aware of how you really feel right now.

C. I AM GOING TO SEE EVERY CORNER OF THE HAUNTED HOUSE!

Picture a homeowner disturbed by noises coming from his tool shed. He decides to investigate. He finds an unlocked window rattling in the wind. Now, where is his concern? It is dissolved in the light of understanding.

The Light of Truth declares, "I am here to heal, not to hurt." The Truth is your friend; it instantly forgives and never condemns. Allow it to circulate into every corner of your mind and Heart. Let it reveal pockets of resistance you did not know were there. Declare, "I am going to see every corner of the haunted house!"

PURPOSE TIP: Any place inside yourself where you feel pain is a place where you are rejecting the entrance of the Light.

D. WHY DID I SAY THAT?

Here is the power of honesty on the spot, and it transforms your life. Detect strained speech and remember: The closer you are to a mistake when you observe it, the more deeply will be your insights and healings. Did I speak just now because I was unaware? Was I anxiously trying to impress? This *NowFact* awakens your curiosity, which is never harsh, but simply wants to observe and learn.

These practical and enjoyable techniques lift you far beyond the pages of a book into the domain of direct experience and revelation. You're learning the art of being your own teacher by jolting awake energies you already possess.

Q & A

Q: What are we trying to accomplish with self-observation?

A: The objective is to learn everything about the mind, which means to observe the mind without self-condemnation. When this is done with calm curiosity, it will not interfere with the performance of daily activities. To become familiar with yourself creates unity, which actually enhances your ability to act with ease and competence. Consciously inhabit the patterns of the mind. Like a ripe fruit that falls from the tree, letting go is effortless when all the nuances of a false pattern are fully revealed.

Q: How does self-observation bring this about?

A: In ancient Egypt, mirrors were placed in underground rooms to catch a single ray of light. This ray was then reflected, using additional mirrors, to endless rooms and levels. As our capacity for self-observation expands we reflect the light into increasingly remote corridors of our psychic system.

We start to see the little things that were previously hidden, such as the quick thoughts of anger or discontent. As our inner world lights up through self-observation, we feel increasingly cheerful, but we are also stunned that so much dust and debris have collected. It seems like a paradox, but the deeper we see into the cellar, the better we feel.

There are three layers for us to look at. The surface layer is pretense, where most people live. The second is the actual layer, the way we really are beneath the pretense. The third is the healing layer. It is possible to leave the surface, travel *through* the actual layer and reach the healing layer.

Q: How can we develop this talent to far higher levels of proficiency?

A: One good way is to tap its power first thing every day. When you wake up in the morning use this *NowFact*, "Time to go to work." Immediately notice as much as you can about yourself. What is your mood? What are your thoughts? What are your feelings? Give yourself this healthy jolt first thing in the morning. When working with the power of self-observation, don't try to hold a psychological disturbance at a distance. When it moves closer to you, don't fight it. Let it increase in intensity. *The closer it gets to you, the more transparent it becomes!* The things we fear draw their seeming power from our attempts to keep them away.

The sincere spiritual student asks Truth to reveal more of the inner darkness. The Truth reveals that darkness is a foreign element with no connection to who you really are. There is great cheerfulness in these insights. False teachings try to evade darkness or cover it up. Real spirituality takes its candle and walks right to the middle of the darkness. The candle turns into a bright blazing light. Light heals. It never condemns. Light is Life.

Q: Self-observation has been compared to a flock of birds crossing the sky. As with thoughts, have we made the mistake of identifying with them and claiming them as our own, instead of just casually observing them and letting them fly by?

A: Yes. Your True Self is not connected to any dark thought that moves through the mind. Darkness is like a dump truck that wants to unload in your yard, but it can do so only if you sign the delivery receipt and accept the trash as yours. Contemplate this principle instead: *Darkness wants you to think it is you who has problems, when in fact it has problems.* The freedom in this principle is beyond words to describe.

PURPOSE TIP: You are the Light;

you are not what it reveals.

Q: What are some additional ways we can apply self-observation?

A: We want to see what we say to ourselves as a result of what we see or hear. One way to do this is to observe precisely your reaction to any given word. How do you react when you first hear the word? For example, someone says, "That was a silly comment." With self-observation present and active, you perhaps detect a quiver of defensiveness to the word "silly." On another occasion, someone says, "That was a brilliant comment." You observe a false reaction of satisfaction over the word "brilliant." How interesting that one little word can spin the gears! The aim is to observe reactions without self-condemnation, as you might watch a band play on stage.

Another effective way to deepen self-observation is to notice associations. For example, you see a woman in a green coat. Be alert to any associative links to someone else you once knew who wore a green coat. Don't be asleep to the mechanical connections that take place in the mind. See them! You will still have mental associations but inner light instantly dissolves any anguish that wants to accompany them. You don't get carried away.

What is your immediate reaction when you first notice someone? When you see a letter or email from them? These quick reactions are what we want to see. Self-observation makes your day rich and fascinating in a way that nothing else can.

Q: What do we do once we have detected the reaction?

A: See as much about it as possible; for example, where does it create physical tension? Every thought is connected to a muscle. Self-observation reveals that a negative thought must grip a muscle in order to linger.

Also, be very alert to the reaction to the reaction. First see the thought, then see the reaction concerning the thought. First there's a critical thought about someone, then there's a reaction to the thought that perhaps says, "I'm a bad person for thinking that thought." Or, first there's a thought about a person of the opposite sex, then there's a thought that reacts to the original thought saying, "I'm unspiritual for thinking that." The light of self-observation heals all of this. We are missing so much!

Q: Does the light itself dissolve the false?

A: Yes! A speaking coach was hired to give advice to a corporate executive who wanted to improve his presentation skills. The coach videotaped the executive giving a talk then played the performance back for him. The executive immediately saw a distracting gesture that he was totally unaware he was doing. He asked the speech coach, "How can I get rid of this? It is so deeply a part of me that I had no idea I'm doing this, and I'm doing it all the time!" The speech coach replied, "You don't have to *do* anything about it. You now are aware of it. Your awareness lets it fall away."

PURPOSE TIP: Don't try too hard with these powerful techniques. Maintain a light-spirited attitude toward your practice, like the enjoyment of playing a new game.

HEART HINTS

1. Self-observation gently familiarizes you with the hidden content of the mind, and in this understanding is your healing.

2. People are often afraid of self-observation because it dissolves the flattering self-picture they have of themselves as being loving and mature, but what a great weight these pictures are!

3. Light goes into your mind's secret recesses and heals, freeing all the originally pure energy it finds there.

4. When we increasingly detect the quick thoughts of anger, discontent, jealousy or comparison, that's good. We're moving in toward the core.

5. Never take your fears, your despairs, or your pains as an enemy. Instead, use them to learn.

6. The *NowFact* "There is _____" is the ideal launching pad for this energy.

7. Self-observation is like the sky. You have all the space you need to understand yourself as the clouds float by.

8. Imagine the relief experienced by the *absence* of self-condemnation over anything you see in yourself.

9. The *NowFact* "How do I *really* feel" takes you through the self-images of how you should feel to the actual content of what you are experiencing right now.

10. There is a space between stimulus and response, and in this space is your rich and purpose-filled life.

Vital Secret #3
INSTANT CHOICE
Free Yourself Now!

The previous energy, Energy #2, employs the patient power of self-observation to gradually dissolve negative moods—the sticky ones that linger in spite of your wish to send them away. But what about the flighty cuckoo thoughts, such as a quick flashback to an embarrassing mistake made years ago or worry over another's opinion of you. These cuckoo thoughts serve no practical purpose. They tug you away from the present moment. You can dismiss them easily with the energy of instant choice.

Mr. Howard gives one of the best descriptions ever of instant choice. He writes in his book, *The Power of Your Supermind*:

A chief cause of unhappiness is what I call mental movies.
Mental movies are a misuse of the imagination.

You know how it goes. You have a painful experience with someone, then run it over and over in your mind. You visualize what you said, what he did, how you both felt. As awful as it is, you feel compelled to repeat the film day and night. It's as if you were locked inside a theater playing a horror movie.

To break out be aware that you *are* running a mental movie. Be conscious of its mechanical hold on your mind. Then, by deliberate choice, break it off. Shake your head and break it off. Now, at this instant, take a quick look. Where is your pain? It is not there. It has disappeared. You have now accomplished something great. You have proved that you *can* snap the film and its tyrannical pain. You are free and you are free *right now*.

Every negative thought carries with it a baton, just like the runners in a relay race. The first runner hands it off to the second runner, and he to the third. Likewise, the preoccupied mind unknowingly consents to negative associations that trigger gloomy moods. With instant choice, awareness steps in and halts the transfer of the baton.

The practical power of *NowFacts* and *The Language of Awakening* must be experienced to be believed. They work wonders because they use the power of internal, silent speech ("In the beginning was the Word . . ." John 1:1) to awaken what your Central Self already knows.

PURPOSE TIP: When you catch yourself caught by wrongness, just switch to the Higher World. When you switch to the Higher World, you will know you are not the person you were just three seconds ago.

Develop your energy of instant choice with these NowFacts:

A. THERE ARE HIGHER THINGS TO THINK ABOUT.

The old way of thinking has its favorite grooves, such as mental arguments with people not present. When you see yourself involved in one of these internal movies, pause and say to yourself: "There are higher things to think about." This *NowFact* snaps the spell and moves you to higher ground.

The mind possesses a natural ability to create mental pictures. The positive side of this power is used when artists see in their mind the finished painting or sculpture. Architects employ this faculty with great precision. It is used in cooking, teaching, business and any place successful projects manifest. The mind thinks in pictures. This is why stories, myths, parables and illustrations inspire for centuries.

The negative use of this power occurs when you're asleep at the switch and allow the mind to fall into energy draining mental movies. It is crucial to wake up and declare, "There are higher things to think about." You'll feel new vitality as the power of instant choice reclaims the energy consumed by these films.

B. I DON'T BELONG HERE.

As you gain a taste for the wholesome and nutritious food served at spiritual banquets, you find that the cotton candy served by lower states of mind taste terrible. After working for awhile with *NowFacts*, Susan K. commented, "Worry and anger taste bitter to me now." I replied, "This is a sure sign of growth! Since Truth has a built-in appeal, the better you feel, the better you *want* to feel."

I don't belong here! This wonderful *NowFact* reminds you that you *do* have the power of choice, and the dry, hot desert of low-level human involvements are not where you belong. Your home is your awakened Heart.

PURPOSE TIP: One thing that determines how much progress you've made is how fast you recover from a blow. Just how soon can you start fresh?

C. I DON'T HAVE TO STRAIN BECAUSE TRUTH IS HERE.

The simple recognition of Truth's presence releases its energy. You instantly receive, without strain and struggle, the insight it possesses. The energy of instant choice expressed in this *NowFact* creates an immediate switch to ease, health and sanity.

A related *NowFact*: "Truth, teach me to relax in spite of myself." Here we have the healthy insight that the old self prefers strain and tension to the cheerful and relaxed flow of spiritual reality. These preferences are habits. You have the power to change your preferences by daring to catch a glimpse of your rich and purpose-filled life.

D. I WANT TO THINK MY OWN THOUGHTS.

Negative thoughts can be instantly dismissed when you clearly understand they are an *imposition*—they are not your own. Your Central Self is thinking wise thoughts now. It has never ceased to do so. These are your real thoughts.

We have been hypnotized by parrots perched in the dark jungle. As we walk past, they sneak in close and squawk in our name. Being oblivious to their presence, we assume the thoughts we hear are our own. "I want to think my own thoughts" is a perfect *NowFact* for activating your power of instant choice.

"I want to think my own thoughts!"

More than a few parrots have become experts in self-improvement and religious subjects. Though they occasionally say something true, it is nonetheless mechanical. In the next paragraph they squawk something from parrot-land. Their talk is far away from matching their walk. "Who you are speaks so loudly I can't hear what you're saying" (Emerson).

When you feel pressure from anyone, anywhere, in person or on television, let that pressure instantly remind you that you have the power of choice. You can pause and remember what a deeper part of you already knows. You can instantly connect with the rich and purpose-filled life that is yours right now. You have the spiritual right to think your own thoughts. This is your inner lighthouse.

Q & A

Q: It seems to me that everything depends on our power of choice. Is that true?

A: The seven energies are attributes of one magnificent unified source. We choose to be in the present, choose to observe ourselves, choose to develop independence and self-reliance. However, our energy of instant choice has been dormant.

The question is, how does one best restore this power? Reading alone can certainly never do it. But there is something we can do that goes right to the core. By making the choice to abruptly exit unproductive streams of thought and hypnotic mental movies when they present themselves, we activate our power of choice and it flourishes in every dimension of life

Instant choice breaks up comfortable patterns with a sudden return to awareness and sanity. It does not allow us to get away with it! How compassionate, and what a loving gift for our development.

Q: Are there any other exercises that can develop instant choice?

A: Here is a wonderful exercise we can call *self-surprise*. It powerfully develops instant choice. Here is how it works:

Picture a railroad car rolling down the tracks toward danger. A switchman is standing beside the tracks with a giant lever in his hand. At the very last moment, he throws the switch and sends the railcar in the direction of safety.

You are about to say something hurtful to another person. The angry statement has left the dock; it is traveling at the speed of light toward the mouth. Instant choice steps in, a spiritual switch is thrown and you do not say what you were about to say. You say something helpful and positive instead. Every time you practice self-surprise you send a healing jolt into the depths of yourself.

You'll instantly feel the trueness of practicing this exercise. Anger did not succeed in dictating your speech. Your power of choice lifted you above anger's arrows. This is not the practice of phony niceness. It is the expression of true strength and authentic self-command. It can occur only when awareness is active in the midst of anger, like the presence of a lighted lodge in the dark forest.

Q: Isn't it true that most people do not want to be jolted?

A: The more advanced a teaching, the more it will refuse to support flattering self-images and counterproductive behavior. With instant choice you can get rightly tough with yourself.

You simply will no longer allow yourself to doze. You *want* to wake up and instant choice is a tremendous catalyst.

Q: How can we realize this?

A: We can! In fact, your Heart knows it now. You can never lose the fact of your present freedom. We're all like fish roaming around in the ocean saying, "Where's the ocean?"

Most of us are preoccupied most of the time. Are you willing to be *unlike* the vast majority? Are you willing to be your awakened Heart in place of what the world wants you to settle for? You can't have both. "How long halt ye between two opinions?" (1 Kings 18:21)

Q: Is instant choice a more deliberate energy than self-observation?

A: Yes. The Taoist refer to life's dance of the yin and the yang—the soft and the hard. Self-observation is a yin energy. It is gentle and receives a gloomy mood as easily as the sky receives a dark cloud. The sky is infinitely greater than the dark cloud, so why be concerned? Why not just let the cloud linger awhile and fade away in its own time? Conversely, instant choice is yang energy. It is more deliberate and determined. You simply refuse to consent to your mind being used as a nest for cuckoos. Don't hesitate to let the energy of instant choice create firm resolve and make you rightly tough with yourself.

While conducting the "SuperWisdom Workshops" I have often been asked, "Do I observe my thoughts or do I interrupt my thoughts?" The answer is, both! We employ Energy #2 (self-observation) at times, and Energy #3 (instant choice) at other times. It is not "either/or." It is much more subtle and comprehensive than that. You alternate and explore.

HEART HINTS:

1. Just as a vibrating rod can be stopped, don't fear to abruptly end unproductive conversations with yourself.

2. The false self wants to recharge; however, your work with the instant choice *NowFacts* denies it the food.

3. Through the process of association, one negativity triggers another, but with *NowFacts* you can choose to interrupt the chain of falling dominoes.

4. If there's any place in your life where bitterness lingers, persistently employ the *NowFact* "There are higher things to think about" and watch with delight how cheerfulness dawns.

5. The *NowFact* "I don't have to strain because Truth is here" reminds us of the need to work with the easy touch and never get stressed out over results from our spiritual practices.

6. Regarding the *NowFact* "I want to think my own thoughts," I'm reminded of how Mr. Howard asked us once, "Why do you have more confidence in other people than you do in yourself? Why do you value what other people think more than you value what you think?"

7. We live in a world of endless zones of pressure exerted by insecure people who want to control our thinking so they can control our behavior.

8. "I don't belong here" certainly applies to physical places but it is 100 times more powerful applied inwardly when we find ourselves drifting in dingy areas of the inner city.

9. Angry or cutting remarks hurt, so derail negative momentum immediately before it leaves the mouth with the self-surprise exercise.

10. False teachers will not challenge you because they want something from you, so be cheerful and grateful over the fact that
you can develop your power to challenge yourself.

Vital Secret #4
INDEPENDENCE
Stop Trying to Please People Who Can't be Pleased

Have you caught a glimpse of how most people don't want you to
change? Those who wish this for you are your true friends. However, most people you know have an image of you in their minds,
like a painting in their living room. When you change, it disturbs
their picture, and they don't like that.

The reason independence is so important is this: You make the
higher discoveries of your Heart firsthand, through your own direct
perception. This means you must find your own way, which ulti-
mately will be an entirely unique way. A sea captain is a captain
precisely because he acts from direct perception of what needs to
be done. His memory *serves him*; he does not serve it. He has his
own style. He is not like any other sea captain in the fleet.

For many years I had the job of training salespeople in the field.
The company paid my expenses to fly to the trainees' hometowns
and show them the ropes. No classroom theoretical training, just
out there doing it. I discovered I could best assist the new employ-
ees by helping them feel comfortable with their own style, their own
method of communicating. For example, one man I worked with
would explain a given aspect of our company's service to the busi-

ness owner, then pause before moving on—I mean pause for a long time. It about drove me crazy at first. But I kept my mouth shut and didn't try to correct him. As he developed his comfort level, the business owners bought! The long pauses were his style!

Genuine spiritual independence grants others space to relax, be themselves and learn and grow. Unlike the dependent, the independent have no wish for conformity. As Mr. Howard writes, "Nature never duplicates a path."

Independence is sacred and, like awareness, it is a theme explored in great depth by all authentic spiritual teachings. For example J. Krishnamurti writes:

> You have to find out what truth is because that is the only thing that matters, not whether you are rich or poor, not whether you are happily married and have children, because they all come to an end. . . . So, without any form of belief, you must find out; you must have the vigor, the self-reliance, the initiative, so that for yourself you know what truth is, what God is . . . The mind can only be free through vigor, through self-reliance.

And Anthony de Mello speaks with challenging directness and clarity when he says:

> Nobody ever rejects you; they're only rejecting what they think you are. But that cuts both ways. Nobody ever accepts you either. Until people come awake, they are simply accepting or rejecting their image of you. They've fashioned an image of you, and they're rejecting or accepting that. See how devastating it is to go deeply into that. It's a bit too liberating.

66

Mr. Howard writes in his classic *The Mystic Path to Cosmic Power*:

Dare to make up your mind about puzzling matters, even if you make a mistake. It is necessary to exercise your own mind, if you are ever to reduce and abolish mistakes. Don't let other people make mistakes for you; have the courage to make your own. A small tree cannot grow to full height, when sheltered by a large tree.

PURPOSE TIP: Independence is not a reaction to authority—it is not a horizontal movement. Independence is *vertical!* It is *transcendence*, which is the loving wish that all real teachings have for you.

With the following NowFacts, *you have the tools to transcend a world that has no desire for you to leave them in their cherished swamp:*

A.THAT IS YOUR FEAR (OR WORRY, PROBLEM, REGRET), NOT MINE.

Dependence causes us to assume that the negative feelings of others belong to us. The energy of independence informs us that negative feelings are present but we do not have to pick them up and churn them around in our system.

We harm people when we take in their negative atmosphere and pass it back to them. We help others and ourselves when we neutralize negativity at the door—*before* it has a chance to enter our thinking. "That is your _____, not mine" also has great power in the inner world as you inform darkness that its worries, problems and regrets are not your own.

A related *NowFact*: "Darkness harbors worry (or regret, or anger or fear) but I do not." Great insight is in this *NowFact*. The only power darkness has is when you accept its falsehood as your own possession.

B. OTHERS ENJOY MY COMPANY TO THE DEGREE I ENJOY MY OWN.

Anytime you see yourself struggling to make a good impression, you can employ this *NowFact* to let go of strained effort and enjoy your own company. A rich and purpose-filled life is found and expressed by inhabiting the domain of your Central Self. This domain is so charming and attractive that even while with others you never leave your own company. This is true kindness that effortlessly benefits others. In fact, it reaches people all over the world with an invisible touch, people you may never know or see personally. Rightness radiates remembrance.

In my old home of Arkansas, while chatting with my nieces and nephews recently, I observed tension and a strained effort to make a favorable impression. I was unknowingly thinking, after all, I'm the uncle. I have a role to play. I let go of all that and resonated this *NowFact* to myself several times. Everything switched. Ease appeared again. I returned to my Central Self and the entire tone of the atmosphere changed for the better.

"The happiness we receive from ourselves is greater than that which we obtain from our surroundings" (Metrodorus).

C. WHO ARE YOU TRYING TO KID?

Once upon a time there was a wise manager who handled the finances of a large corporation. People constantly approached him with unnecessary requests for money—$50,000 for this project, $70,000 for that one. He looked at them and said, "Who are you trying to kid?"

This *NowFact* informs negative inner states that the power they had at one time, they no longer possess. Said silently to others, it conveys the same message. It is not said from a feeling of superiority or with an ounce of hostility. It is simply stated as the bright fact that it is.

PURPOSE TIP: The energy of independence
develops an immediate recognition of
elements foreign to your new nature.

Boldly inform darkness with *The Language of Awakening* that a new day has dawned. Darkness is a clever bluffer and is trying to discourage you before too much light is turned on, and it will have to depart since it won't be able to stand it.

Negativity observed in its infancy is easily dissolved when you wisely ask, "Who are you trying to kid?" Here are three more related *NowFacts*:

1. "You've got the wrong man/woman."
2. "I am no longer who you think I am."
3. "That may have worked at one time, but no more."

D. IF YOU KNOW WHAT IS BEST FOR ME,
WHY ARE YOU SO MISERABLE?

Those who are the least able to manage their own lives are the ones most eager to manage yours. To call a halt to their pernicious and determined efforts to dominate your thinking, a direct and highly concentrated *NowFact* is necessary.

Though your outer demeanor will be firm and resolute, inwardly you'll be consciously tender toward the offender. There is not a speck of hostility or self-righteousness when this *NowFact* is voiced silently within from pure perception. You'll know with 100 percent clarity that behind the delusional controller's hard and brittle façade is a great cave of anguish. This insight is true compassion.

Such mature and truly spiritual conduct on your part may be the one chance the bulldozer has to break the painful pattern and begin to recover. Maybe he or she will ask one day, "What's this? Here's someone who's not afraid. I wonder why?"

E. I AM GOING TO LEARN TO LIVE WITHOUT YOU 100 PERCENT.

This silent statement has a specific application. It is directed to that strained smile that appears when you try to appease someone, or gain their approval. Calmly yet firmly inform these tense facial muscles, "I am going to learn to live without you 100 percent."

You'll have many opportunities to use this statement to develop authentic independence. As a result, your inner world is much more at ease and the quality of your relationships rises. Again, there is no anger or self-condemnation directed toward the strained smile, but simply an intelligent statement of fact. You *are* going to learn to live without that strained "like me" smile 100 percent. It is your destiny because this strength is within you now. You just needed a tool to use that is stronger than the strained smile. Now you have it!

Unproductive patterns need to be informed of the truth on the spot, and *NowFacts* are the ideal way for you to do so. A related *NowFact*: "I am going to own my own life, and I'm going to start with my face."

PURPOSE TIP: When your face is as relaxed and alert as the wise and cheerful thoughts circulating in your Heart, your relationships are transformed.

F. JUST A MINUTE. WHOSE LIFE IS THIS?

You have a right to your energy, time and attention. It is never selfish to live your life as you see fit; it is selfish only to insist that other people live as you see fit.

We have responsibilities to nurture our children and perform our daily work with reliability and efficiency. However, when we take responsibility for things *adults* must do for themselves, we rob them of the chance they have to develop. Much evil is done in the name of "helping" people. You owe nothing to adults except a mature mind and spirit, and they owe nothing to you but the same.

A related *NowFact*: "I can choose to live in the light when around lovers of darkness." Even though you may have to work next to someone who embraces the desert, *you* can choose the oasis. You can refuse to participate in gossip, chuckle at crude jokes or condone immature behavior. You can live in the light without harboring feelings of superiority. It is not negative or judgmental to see that someone is a lover of darkness. They can change their choice, but they must claim this power for themselves, just as you are working to do.

PURPOSE TIP: Never forget: You have a right to *your* choice! It can be taken from you only if you give it away.

Be wise and avoid letting desert dwellers see how much you know about them. Simple politeness is a virtue for its own sake, but it also helps you keep inner-life insights private. Christ said it with the utmost brevity: "Don't cast your pearls before swine" (Matthew 7:6).

Q & A

Q: Is it true that society wants us dependent and compliant?

A: Absolutely it is true. Emerson spoke well when he said "Society everywhere is in conspiracy against the manhood of every one of its members."

To live in the higher state of oneness revealed in all true spiritual literature, we must first see how dependent we are. We must face the shocking revelations of how easily our thinking is swayed by the world's opinions and fads, even facial expressions.

The more a person talks about his independence, the less he or she is likely to actually have it. We must let the facts jolt us out of dependency.

It may sound surprising, but you can use television to develop independence! When you're watching a movie or the late breaking news, snap the spell. In the middle of that exciting scene on the screen, look away. Reclaim your attention. Take a deep breath. Strike a blow for independence by practicing this exercise often. Simple practices like this spark these vast powers to life.

Q: How does empathy connect with independence?

A: While absorbing the cheerful feelings that exist in higher spiritual states, we develop a powerful sense of contrast. As we begin to more quickly detect our own slips into unproductive desert areas of the mind, we increasingly perceive the inner states of people around us.

When people are preoccupied, they can walk into a room of people where negative feelings are present and wrongly believe that these negative feelings originated within themselves. As we grow, we perceive that the negative feelings of others are *their* feelings. We're aware that negativity is present, but we do not take it as being our own. Growing independence creates empathy and the ability to consciously put yourself in another person's place, without getting personally involved with what you perceive.

Let's again look at the synergy. The energy of self-observation creates independence from negative thoughts revealing clear open spaces within, which are gradually filled with higher feelings. This produces a contrast between the awakened state and the preoccupied state and in turn nourishes the power of empathy—the ability to stay in your own brightness while simultaneously discerning the inner states of others.

Q: Why is there an unseen fear of independence? Is it because we must then think for ourselves?

A: Yes. It connects to the fear of making mistakes and being criticized for them. Some, or much of this, we picked up in childhood. We can transcend all of this.

Here's a personal example. In my earlier years of learning to fly, the day came for my first solo flight. We were doing "touch and go" practice landings in which you immediately take off without stopping. After a good landing my instructor Wally said, "Tom, pull over there. I need to get something." He stepped out on the wing of the Piper Warrior, looked back in and said, "Take her for a few rounds, and I'll see you when you get back." What! Alone!

A few weeks later Wally said, "Fly over to North Little Rock" (about seven miles away). What! Alone! Leave my now familiar and cherished airport pattern? Next came my first cross-country flight from Little Rock, Arkansas, to Memphis, Tennessee, some 120 miles away. All I had to do was follow the interstate down there, but getting that far away from my home base was nerve-racking.

After several years of experience I undertook the IFR training—the "Instrument Flight Rules" where you learn to fly in bad weather by using the instruments alone. It was a tremendous challenge in the beginning to land a plane in fog and rain. I was afraid, but gradually it became easier.

Fear clings to the familiar. It pulls out its big guns just before a breakthrough. Fear is predictable; it's always going to object! But fear is a bluff. We learn by experience that shaking is harmless *if we keep walking.*

Q: Can you say more about how independence leads to harmonious relationships?

A: The energy of independence develops empathy. It's not that you're reading another's thoughts; rather, your essence connects with the truth in another. It's like the strings on a guitar. When you pluck one string, the others vibrate in harmony with it. If you do not strike your own harmonious chords, the world will make you dance to its tune.

Q: Can you talk more of independence within the setting of spiritual groups?

A: When we fall back on any small or large institution as our principle authority, we water the seeds of rigidity and failure. Such dependency may appear right and some argue that "new people" need it, but we never strengthen our self-reliance by giving it away.

The wisdom seeker who treasures independence can profitably participate in a group and not get caught by all the undercurrents, even in a rare group of genuine value. Always remember that a true teacher encourages independence and self-reliance.

Q: So many groups and organizations exist today. Some of the leaders are quite dynamic. What's going on?

A: False teachers like the big show of followers, meetings, buildings and money, which are enticing to the ego. Sufi writer Idries Shah tells us in *The Commanding Self* what happens:

> The blind cannot lead the blind. Generally such
> organizations become soaked in self-esteem and lose
> humility. Few Christian leaders today would accept Jesus,
> for instance, if they met him. Instead of really knowing
> anything, they feed upon self-esteem, which develops
> into what we call the "Commanding Self." It is very

terrible, because this is diametrically opposed to their real possible destiny.

"Soaked in self esteem" that's very important. The "I was a favored student of a great teacher" attitude has definitely sunk many ships.

Also remember that not all of the wise are out writing books or conducting classes. Like Dr. Chapin, they are perfectly content to light their own corner of the world, knowing that by spiritual law the light will always find its way; it cannot be contained.

Q: How do we prevent an authentic spiritual teaching from turning rigid and programmed, as if it can fit in a belief structure?

A: Let's stay with Idries Shah on this:

> If you have any experience with spiritual groups, you
> will know that too many people focus their attention on
> the teacher and not on the teaching. Indeed, this is such
> a frequent abuse that some people become completely
> fixated on a teacher, whether true or false.

Truth flows like Niagara Falls. The aim is never the book or the teacher or the organization. *The aim is the waterfall they point to!* Some have let themselves get blocked by overlooking this fact in their actions, even though they may say they agree with it.

One more thing before we move on. The ego loves to take a vital spiritual truth and twist it to maintain its position such as the truth of the necessity for independence. It's upsetting to the ego to entertain the idea that someone knows more than it does. In fact, the ego often wants to move from student to teacher as soon as possible, in record time if it can.

PURPOSE TIP: The middle path is the answer—a willingness to concede someone knows more and there's something to learn, without sacrificing one ounce of one's self-reliance.

Q: It's refreshing to hear these truths stated so directly. Do many authors and speakers hold back because they're afraid they'll offend?

A: Yes indeed. We have good manners here. The Truth is gentle and kind, yet its standards are very high. It both encourages what is true in us and rebukes what is false. Truth is not going to lower itself to win the favor of anyone.

HEART HINTS

1. "Be your own person, think with your own mind, stand on your own two feet" (Dr. Chapin).

2. Increasingly, you enjoy being alone with your real nature, but when with others, you are socially competent and at ease. You are not shy and withdrawn because you aren't trying to find someone to be nicer to you than you are to yourself.

3. These truths can sometimes seem hard and uncaring, as with

the silent *NowFact* "If you know what is best for me, why are you so miserable?" but they are in fact the exact opposite; they are filled with compassion.

4. Drop anxious searching for a teacher—let Truth teach you.

5. Independence is a higher state of learning because it is receptive and flexible; it is free of the desire to conform and please.

6. Independence teaches us that the wise and happy thoughts of the Heart are more rewarding and interesting than anything the world can present, which makes it possible to enjoy the world in a whole new way.

7. There is a symphony being played in the Heart, but we're asleep to its melodies because the mind is now so noisy.

8. The *NowFact* "That is your _____, not mine" reminds you a spiritual law exists that says the trash adults make for themselves must be cleaned up by them.

9. The more independence you have, the more you detect and avoid subtle pressure such as "Get nervous like me."

10. Real spiritual growth is its own evidence. You know it is happening. You see what is beginning inside of you.

Vital Secret #5
FORGIVENESS
How to Deal With Yourself and Your Mistakes

Medical science has proven that letting go of blaming others for the harm we believe they have done has definite benefits for health and well-being. Nothing crushes like grudges.

But there is a far higher level of forgiveness. It includes the understanding that we live in a gigantic stage production, that actors appear and disappear, that good fortune is as much of a hoax as bad fortune. It also includes the understanding that the characters are scripted. They are asleep inside the production. Until we wake up from the dream, we cannot act above the level of the script.

Shakespeare most definitely realized this higher view when he said, "All the world's a stage, and all men and women merely players."

Here's an illustration: In the late 1800s a man's photograph was placed in the saddlebag of a Pony Express rider and mailed on a long journey across the country. At one point it was lost and left out in a rainstorm, then transferred to a smoky train. What if the person who sent the photograph thought the photo was actually himself? He would be upset, indignant and deeply concerned over the scratches and blemishes.

The moral of the lesson: *The picture is not you.* From a small child we develop a self-image. Like everyone around us, we learn to defend and promote the image. When it is rejected by others, we develop a grudge against them. When it is accepted and flattered, we call them "friends." This roller coaster becomes our "life."

The answer is to dissolve the pictures through self-honesty and all the wonderful principles you're discovering in this book. When you know the picture is not you, anything can happen to it and you're okay. Remember this fabulous principle and use it as a *NowFact*: "It happened, but it did not happen to me."

In Reality, there is no separate self there apart from the whole of Life. What is there is simply a collection of every painful experience and painful thought. But this collection of pain is not you. Yes, it is there, but there is no self present to whom it belongs. This thought is remarkably freeing.

What holds the pained self together is the conviction there is an actual person there who is suffering. Yes, there have been painful experiences. But none of these painful experiences ever happened to you!

Living from these lofty facts enhances your ability to fulfill your roles and responsibilities in life. When immersed in the big production, we fall for the ups and downs and lose our Center. Forgiveness dawns as we realize our oneness with the Source of Life.

Here is how to place vast currents of rejuvenation to work for you, and experience the wonders of forgiveness on an entirely new level:

A. NOW IS NEW!

A mistake of 50 years ago or five seconds ago has no legal claim on the present. Who you *really* are never fell asleep, never made the mistake. The power of the present moment is so immense it is capable—when lived in fully—of destroying forever every past mistake and regret.

The power of "now is new" is beyond words to describe. You can use this *NowFact* often to recover after any misstep, whether large or small. Recovery *is* forgiveness as you learn the lesson and cheerfully move on.

PURPOSE TIP: "While on the path to complete freedom, we learn a lot through our own errors. Errors are always stepping-stones to one who walks the path of truth."

—*Dr. Chapin*

B. I AM HERE TO LEARN.

The spiritual path gets more difficult, yet in other ways it gets easier. It is easier because we're closer to our Central Self and its endless supply of wisdom and refreshment, yet it is more difficult in that to grow Life brings about new and often challenging experiences. We are not here for comfort or soothing. Leave that to the false teachers. We're here to wake up from the gigantic dream and rediscover our rich and purpose-filled life. "I am here to learn."

For example, an exceptionally difficult person may appear in our life after years of study. This is an opportunity to learn. It teaches us self-command and jolts us out of complacent patterns. Yet, how often do we let our self-images take over and resist the lesson with whispers like,"You're a spiritual person. You don't need this." The fact is that it might be precisely what we need.

At the same time this is true, it is also true that you need never consent to another person treating you badly. What to do is never cast in stone. Every situation is different. Our aim is flexibility. With the *NowFact* "I am here to learn" you can go against what the false pattern wants in favor of what is truly best for you.

Here's another *NowFact*: "The only reason I made a mistake

is because I did not understand something. Since it is possible to acquire the needed understanding, I will do so."

PURPOSE TIP: If you are tempted and fail, just learn from the experience. Don't condemn yourself. Just see and learn.

C. I AM AWAKE AND I AM IN CHARGE!

When you feel yourself drifting with the hypnosis of society, when your thinking is scattered, pause and say to yourself: "I am awake and I am in charge!" This is an entirely different "I" than the one asleep just a moment ago. Now, flow with this new state for as long as possible. Be alert to any guilt thought that tries to condemn you for having been asleep.

You are instantly forgiven for having been preoccupied just a second ago. Don't let darkness trick you into self-condemnation over having been vacant, even if you were vacant for hours. Step past this sly trick and stay awake. "Now is new!"

A related *NowFact* is "I want to live!" When tempted by a grudge, self-accusation, anger or worry, step beyond it *now* by declaring with heartfelt intensity, "I want to live!"

D. TIME TO TAKE THE NEXT STEP UP!

Forgiveness is a step up and out of the dozing old self to a new place of learning and receptivity. You will gain great enthusiasm as you perceive that every experience, every challenge, can be an opportunity to employ a *NowFact*. This means even a state of anxiety or worry can be an opportunity to "take the next step up." You can use it to turn toward the inner oasis instead of tossing sand around in the desert.

Because the fundamental law of life is growth, "Time to take the next step up!" instantly harmonizes your intent with the universe.

Q & A:

Q: Grudges can run deep! They are persistent and keep bobbing up. How can we find lasting forgiveness at the core of our being?

A: Here's an advanced truth. True forgiveness comes when you comprehend with absolute clarity that no independently operating self is there, apart from God/Truth/Reality, that needs to be forgiven. The false self is an illusion, a vapor; it does not exist to be forgiven and seeing this is forgiveness.

Q: This is a difficult truth. How can I accept it?

A: It is a seed that sprouts and reveals its endless meaning when you let it play lightly on the edges of the mind, then move effortlessly in toward the core. You need not try to figure it out.

Q: Guilt permeates society. It is persistent and seems to never give up. How can I be free of this?

A: Entire religious empires and dishonest charities are built on guilt. It is a favorite weapon of a malicious society as it tries to extract allegiance, money, time and attention from its unaware members. Guilt wails, "Look what you did to me!" We must go beyond dissolving the guilt to dissolving the fictitious guilty person. The false self thrives on having an identity and being a "guilty person" will suit it just fine.

Once we begin to catch glimpses of these deeper truths, we touch rejuvenating currents that heal the illusion of separation. The power of forgiveness is so comprehensive that the false self is dissolved *at the core.*

Q: It's challenging. The magnitude is overwhelming. Do others feel this?

A: We all go through it. Christ said, "He that loseth his life . . . shall find it" (Mathew 10:39). Incredibly, the spiritually blind read this without a trace of discernment. They tell us this applies to the "afterlife," whatever that is. No, it is about dissolving the false life and the resurrection of your true life.

Q: How does forgiveness connect with our relationships?

A: What you want in your Heart is healing for yourself. You desire full recovery and restoration. As your wish for these spiritual treasures deepens, you'll naturally want the same for others, even those who may have appeared to cause you harm. This is not sentimentality. It is sound spiritual truth. At the same time you will know that it is wrong to allow anyone to behave badly toward you. If they insist on doing so, the relationship ends. But this firmness on your part can be present without a trace of bitterness. You want the offender to recover, just as you want recovery for yourself.

We cannot chain others in our own thoughts and expect to be free. In freeing others we free ourselves.

Here are marvelous words from Mr. Howard's book *Pathways to Perfect Living:*

> Forgiveness is not necessarily a matter of going to these people, but of psychic understanding. You must forgive yourself for being spiritually asleep; this is possible when you see things as they really are. This pardons you from every offense you have ever committed, for you knew not what you did; you were out of your true mind. Forgiveness has nothing to do with the offended person; it is solely a matter of your own awakening. This will become increasingly clear to you.

Q: What additional exercises can we practice to develop the power of forgiveness?

A: Before dealing with any crisis or situation that confronts you use this wonderful *NowFact*: "I will handle this the best I know how, yet at the same time I will know there is a much higher way to handle it." The challenge or crisis is there, yes, and it must be dealt with. Do the best you can with your present level of understanding, while knowing there is always more to learn.

Q: So we can forever end self-condemnation?

A: With *The Language of Awakening*, yes we can! Here is another *NowFact* which centers around the word "however." Use it often. Whenever you are in a negative inner state, let "however" remind you there is a higher world. For example, say to yourself something like, "There is worry over this problem; 'however' I choose to remember that tension is unnecessary." When there is a mistake, let it remind you that "now is new." "However" nourishes forgiveness as well as your power of instant choice.

Q: So forgiveness is very much connected to awareness and present moment living?

A: Absolutely. Once again we see the inspiring symmetry of the seven vital secrets. Self-condemnation is the glue that holds the false self together. It is the Source of Life itself—flowing through the present moment—that renews, heals and forgives. Grudges against others melt away, like the images on the theatre screen dissolve when the room's light is turned on.

HEART HINTS

1. The present moment untangles the delusion of a separate self, and authentic forgiveness flourishes.

2. You may be able to forgive others for the harm they have caused you, but can you forgive yourself for the harm you have caused others?

3. You need not "try" and forgive someone because it can strengthen the ego; just tap into the cosmic energy of forgiveness that exists right now.

4. The *NowFact* "now is new" has lofty energy; the more you let it dwell in your thinking, the more you feel its amazing power.

5. The process of growth is like peeling away the layers of an onion. Be patient and let the healing powers do their work.

6. God/Truth/Reality is untouched by every human mistake since the beginning of time, so self-punishment over mistakes is the ultimate waste of energy.

7. The *NowFact* "I am awake and I am in charge" is a bold step toward reclaiming your life, especially when you let "I" resonate in the corridors of your Heart.

8. Having no existence in reality, the false self must continually "repair" and prop itself up with petty grudges; self-condemnation is a grudge turned inward.

9. The rejuvenating currents of forgiveness and recovery seek to heal the Heart, not the intellect, for once the Heart is healed, the mind naturally follows.

10. Self-condemnation is a superglue that repairs any "damage" happiness and insight do to the false self. Dare not to repair it. Let the false self fade away.

Vital Secret #6
EFFICIENCY
Enter Life's Easy Flow

Your Central Self has many positive qualities, including joy, regeneration, gratitude and sufficiency. This is the very thing Christ referred to when he counseled, "Put the kingdom of heaven first, and all these things shall be added unto you" (Luke 12:21). We could rephrase this to say, "Put your Heart foremost and its endless supply of energy nourishes every dimension of your life and experience."

PURPOSE TIP: When pure energy flows directly
into your life, without detours, your life and
your environment blossom like springtime.

It is like the man who is gone for two weeks and returns home to find all his appliances running. While he was away someone broke in and turned everything on. Now that he is back (now that you are aware), wasted energy is reclaimed.

People concern themselves with inefficiency at their desk or in their daily life. A far greater inefficiency—in fact, the one that fuels all the others—is carelessness with our life energy when we divert it to worry, guilt, tension, anger, jealousy and other negative emotions.

You have an abundance of energy. Your Center is pouring forth an endless and inexhaustible supply. It takes patience and persistence, but *you can master* how this energy is deployed. *This is wisdom.*

Look at the symmetry of the seven energies! Energy #1, aware-ness, is absolutely necessary for efficiency. It all starts with the present moment. Energy #2, self-observation, enters as we detect how we waste energy, especially within our own psychic system. Energy #5, instant choice, plays a crucial role as we make new deci-sions on how to deploy this energy. We reclaim our life energy for higher aims.

There is an extremely powerful spiritual energy coming down to earth. It is used by all human beings. But almost everyone uses the energy wrongly, causing enormous pain and tension. The energy is abundant. It we don't harmonize with it, we allow ourselves to be pained by a lack of understanding.

Use these NowFacts in the midst of your daily life to build order and efficiency and keep your energy pure:

A. I CAN HAVE A PROBLEM-FREE NATURE.

Here's a *NowFact* for contemplation in free moments during your day. It contains vast treasures of wisdom and happiness that may not be immediately apparent. Remember, the false self needs con-flict to exist, but *you* do not.

Picture a house filled with old crystal glassware. As cars and trucks pass by, the glasses vibrate. They resonate to the many activi-ties occurring outside the house.

Does it make sense to try to control the outside activities so things will quiet down inside the house? Or, is it far wiser to box up the old glasses and cart them away?

We waste a lot of energy trying to mold people and events to fit our demands. One of the most painful demands is to insist that people behave on a higher level than they actually occupy. Someone can *raise* his level, but until he does, he cannot *act* above that level. False expectations for mature conduct from immature people drain enormous quantities of energy.

Dr. Chapin adds, "We find the true self quickly when we let all things be as they are and let life happen as it will." Once your inner home is clear of vibrating demands, Truth inhabits you with its highly efficient and problem-free nature.

B. I REFUSE TO ALLOW THE THEFT OF MY ENERGY.

Like a pickpocket, whose aim is to divert your attention so he can steal your money, an empty and hungry world lusts after your attention, money and time.

Be especially alert to the tactics of *false positives*. These are usually people who have known you for awhile. When they see changes in your demeanor, they want to find out what's going on. They ask questions and seem interested, not from a real desire to better their lives, but to pry into yours. Be aware of their prying questions and politely refuse.

Your energy is a gift for *your* development. It is not the property of false patterns, whether in yourself or in others. Once you begin to really understand this, you will say with great emotion: "I refuse to allow the theft of my energy!"

A related *NowFact*: "Enough is Enough!" Enough of this nonsense, this appeasement, this disorder! This statement is finality, which is one of the great rewards of the awakened life. *Finality is freedom.*

PURPOSE TIP: Keep your studies simple.
Think clearly, think briefly. Don't complicate
things. You want to get to the point!

C. WHAT A DREADFUL WASTE OF ENERGY THAT COULD BE USED FOR SELF-AWAKENING.

A huge amount of energy is lost in negative emotions. Anger, for example, is a terrible energy thief, an anchor that prevents your ship from moving with the wind. When anger appears within you or in others, it is the perfect time to pause and say: "What a dreadful waste of energy that could be used for self-awakening."

Physical tension consumes a great amount of energy; unaware people have little kinesthetic awareness. Money is an expression of energy and can be wasted in foolish spending. Time is an expression of energy and its wise use is essential for inner development.

We're social creatures and talking with others fills a natural need, but beware of gossip. It dissipates energy like few things can. You can also use this *NowFact* with great effectiveness when you hear gossip disguised as "genuine concern" or a "wish to understand." Gossip is insidious, a dreadful waste of energy and an enticing drug. It leads to slander and the scarring of the soul. When faced with these things, instantly turn toward what your spirit knows is true and decent and clean! If possible, cut all connections to any chronic slanderer/gossiper.

D. I HAVE NOTHING TO SAY TO THAT.

Here are gems from Mr. Howard's booklet *Conquer Anxiety and Frustration*:

> The first step is to remain alert when people try to weigh you down with their nervous comments and attitudes. You will have plenty to observe, for the whole world staggers under the burden of its own gloom.
>
> The next step is to reply to the attempted attack: *I have nothing to say to that.* This cuts off the contagious

effect of the negative assault. It blocks your tendency to accept and imitate depressing words from others. Your nature does not fall to the level of the anxious remark, but remains high above it.

Negative people *want* to get you involved with their defeat, and this is a major method they use to do it. Your reply: *I have nothing to say to that* prevents them from drawing you in as their victim. An attitude of defeat in another person cannot touch you unless you carelessly accept it as yours. And there is no need at all for you to accept it. A quiet refusal to enter the battlefield is the perfect reply.

Here's a related *NowFact*: "Regardless of how I feel about it, that wolf does not belong to me." This reminds you of your power of choice. Picture someone who brings a wolf on a leash to your door. He says, "I found your wolf and I'm returning it to you." You sternly inform the visitor that you own no wolf and quickly shut the door.

PURPOSE TIP: When a negative reaction stands at the doorway of your mind, nothing requires you to invite it in and show it your electrical outlet.

Q & A

Q: We work, run businesses and raise families. Or perhaps we're retired and have other activities and duties. There is such an obvious need for efficiency and clear thinking in everyday affairs. I remember you saying once, "Doing your work right in the world expands your mental powers, allowing you to rise from there to spiritual powers." Yet so many of us on the spiritual path often have our heads in the clouds. How can spirituality and practical thinking develop together?

A: The right use of the mind can be compared to a man who owns two houses. One house is near the road, where all the traffic is. His second house is on a hill behind the lower house. A path goes from the lower house to the higher house. It is very quiet in the upper house. There is none of the noise that exists at the lower house. Likewise, we have a mind to use for practical purposes, but we also have a higher house.

The purpose of life is to use everything to develop the higher house. You then alternate back and forth. You have things to do and think about. But when you are through with practical thought, you put it aside and go up to your higher house.

As we live now, we alternate between practical thought and negative internal rambling. With spiritual growth that changes. We alternate between practical thought and higher awareness.

In the *SuperWisdom Subscription Website* we have a section devoted to proven resources for efficiency, including the 80/20 principle. (80 percent of our results come from just 20 percent of our actions.) Efficiency is a highly profitable study for students of these themes.

Q: How can we develop more focus?

A: Here's another illustration: There was once a man who worked in an office. He was productive, happy and a pleasure to be

95

around. One day an employee mentioned this remarkable co-worker to his manager. "I wonder what makes him different?" The manager replied, "I know what it is. I have studied him for a long time. He stays focused on the essential and free of the unnecessary. I have given the man a nickname. I call him "The man who can leave things alone.""

Q: I like that! How can we be like that man?

A: The original disturbance is not the problem. It is our *reaction* to the disturbance that drains away our energy. Likewise, other people's behavior is not my problem at all. The problem is how I *react* to the actions of others.

Hence, never condemn another person. Never despise them or think bad of them in any way. If you do, you are simply placing yourself where they are. Never hate society. Simply understand. It is your complaints against other people and circumstances that keep in place the conditions you complain about.

When we leave things alone we keep our internal space free and clear. We're open to influences from Truth that have matched every step we take toward it with a step toward us.

Q: Dependence would certainly be a major source of loss of energy. Can you comment on it?

A: There is a certain kind of person who wants to have his life taken over by circumstances, people and events. Not knowing what to do with himself, his life is not his own but belongs to everything that happens to him.

Then there is another kind of very rare person who wants to own his own life and his own energy. He does not surrender his mind to intruders. He is on guard to catch foreign and destructive thoughts, and refuses to allow them to wreck his feelings. He maintains the integrity of his inner world, treasures his power of choice and is selective and discriminating over what he allows to enter the corridors and closets of his mind. He knows the supreme value of energy and refuses to waste it.

Be this rare person! You will have nothing in common with the billions who have given their life away to whatever comes along. They love distraction; you love awareness. You may have to work beside them, but you can be 100 percent detached from them psychologically and spiritually.

Q: What specific way can someone notice an energy-draining dependence in daily life?

A: Here's a good one. Observe people in an elevator. One person stares up at the floor indicator. The others join in. Everyone stares, unaware of what they are doing. People mechanically do what others are doing. Don't be like them. Live your own life! Make your own decisions, even in the smallest things—not from a defiant or go-it-alone attitude, but simply because you want your life to be truly self-directed so you can be of maximum benefit to yourself and others.

Q: I know I should be a more efficient person. How can I?

A: Here's that old "should" again. I'm convinced that if there's a sign over the entrance to Hades, it would read, "You *should* have been more spiritual."

When you organize your home and office, you are expressing the energy of efficiency. When you determine to have more order in your life, you are merging with this energy. This change of viewpoint makes all the difference! Instead of trying to make yourself an "efficient person," you realize that the energy of efficiency already exists.

At the same time, a certain degree of intelligent effort is required to move ourselves out of familiar patterns. The principle "let go and go with the flow" is true, but first we have to see an old pattern in action and let insight lift us out of it. *NowFacts* are ideal for this. They activate instead of indoctrinate.

Simply notice inner or outer energy drainers the moment they appear. Insight *is* action. When you see something clearly there is no waffling on what to do. Also notice how energy conserved expresses itself in constructive decisions and actions, as well as higher levels of creativity. You get more done and the quality is richer.

HEART HINTS

1. The *NowFact* "I have nothing to say to that" is your ticket to freedom from this world's nuttiness, and how beautifully it applies inwardly as you have nothing to say to fear, loneliness or guilt.

2. People who love the swamp are not going to leave it, and your *demand* that they leave it is a dark method carefully orchestrated to get *you* back to the swamp.

3. We must be alert to "false positives" pretending to have an interest in what we're doing so they can plant sinister seeds of doubt and confusion. Talk about the path to a rich and purpose-filled life only with those who show *persistent* interest.

4. Physical tension is a profitable area of inquiry because false patterns like to grip muscles to further their hold.

5. Reclaimed energy begins to circulate in your Heart where increasing vitality releases more. "For whosoever hath, to him shall be given, and he shall have more abundance" (Matthew 13:12).

6. Gossip is insidious and especially dangerous in spiritual groups where it's rationalized with, "We're observing and discussing in order to grow."

7. Be the man or woman who can leave things alone, who feels no obligation or compulsion to pick up junk.

8. When people neglect their spiritual development, they descend ever more deeply into a state of *complaint*.

9. Like awareness and forgiveness, the energy of efficiency is present *now* and need not be created. It simply needs to be recognized.

10. Efficiency with money and time leads to efficiency with your life energy.

Vital Secret #7
RECEPTIVE REQUEST
How to Remember What You Already Know

A receptive request is directed to a power higher than the intellect. This energy can be developed right in the midst of your daily life. Never forget that the power of a prayer is never determined by its length, but by your sincerity.

Also remember to feel these requests resonate through your entire Being. It's not the head that prays with sincerity, but your Central Self. Let your Heart speak.

Cultivate Energy #7 in the midst of daily life with these NowFact prayers:

A. GOD HELP ME.

To multiply the amount of help you receive from this simple request, understand that the *me* you're talking about is not a problem-laden entity separated from the whole of life. It is the part of you that wishes to learn and unfold.

See yourself as someone who wants to learn. This self-view is accurate and in harmony with the deepest laws of life. Truth's help to *who you really are* is instantaneous. "I and my Father are one" (John 10:30). This means my wish to learn and my Inner Teacher are one and the same.

Dr. Chapin adds, "There will be times when you will be guided to ask for physical help and other times your inner voice will tell you, 'Wait . . . Do not hurry . . . This will disappear.' Guidance comes a little here and a little there. When you think it is absent you are mistaken."

Mr. Howard later added a few words to this *NowFact*: "God help me, and help me mean it." These additional five words contain the honest insight that we often ask for help without really meaning it.

B. TRUTH, PLEASE MAKE EVERYTHING CLEAR TO ME.

We need not thrash around and struggle, or be greedy and grasping toward Truth. It is like the familiar Taoist illustration of the muddy pond. When left alone the pond starts to settle and is soon clear. Anxiously trying to *fix* a problem *is* the muddy pond. Clarity is in the Truth itself, and the more we enter into Truth the more its clarity enters into us.

Dr. Chapin adds, "Now do not study too intensely. The study of reality comes to you—you do not need to reach for it. You learn by relaxing, by listening, not by grasping outward. Simply be still and let God do His work."

C. HEAVEN, YOU GIVE ME THE STRENGTH AND I'LL GIVE YOU THE CREDIT.

As we let good things happen without taking personal credit, the energy of the Higher World increasingly inhabits us. Christ said it so simply and beautifully, "Not my will, but thine, be done" (Luke 22:42).

Let's look for a moment at the directive from the Old Testament, "Thou shalt not steal." There's a far higher meaning to these words. It's not necessarily about stealing physical objects. To steal is to attempt to enclose the Spirit of Life within a fictitious identity and to claim credit for creating positive conditions.

"Heaven, you give me the strength and I'll give you the credit" places you in harmony with your Heart so the best can be expressed *through* you. This is a master key to a rich and purpose-filled life.

A related *NowFact*: "Truth will be (fill in the blank) for me." For example, Truth will be *strength* for me, Truth will be *honesty* for me,

Truth will be *clear-mindedness* for me. Place any virtue you wish to express in the blank space.

PURPOSE TIP: Virtues flow with the winds; they are never the isolated property of individual ships.

D. MORE, PLEASE, OF WHATEVER I NEED!

Spiritual Intelligence advances by plateaus. Over and over again you must leave what you think you know and be a beginner on the next level. Two years, ten years, twenty years into the spiritual journey, will you be willing to let the wisdom you've gathered lift you to an entirely new level of understanding? Will you be willing to set aside any heavy self-pictures of being an "advanced student" and be a beginner all over again? This is what the next plateau requires.

Sometimes the next plateau is preceded by a whopper. If you're not making some mistakes, chances are you're living too cautiously.

"More, please, of whatever I need!" helps you request what is truly good for you—not what keeps intact the settled self that thinks it knows so many things. Spiritual Intelligence is oneness with Life. Oneness has no container. What is valuable for awakening your Heart are the challenging experiences that shatter the illusory container.

We cling to what we know in fear of the unknown. Eventually we learn that the unknown is a wonderful place to be. It is the doorway to ever higher lessons. It is our friend and teacher.

E. WOULD THIS BOTHER THE KING?

Use this simple request often, like in snarling traffic or when a little twinge of irritation appears over the waiter being late with the food. Use it also for big problems such as relationships, health or money. Would these things upset Truth? Action may be required, but would this bother the spiritual King? The answer always energizes you!

Sometimes things break apart on this level. People with whom you socialized or worked together for years are no longer in your life, for whatever reason. Just know that a new chapter is before you. The King is not at all concerned.

If I had to choose ten favorite Vernon Howard quotes, this one from *Esoteric Encyclopedia of Eternal Knowledge* would be one of them:

> Look at change from a totally new viewpoint. You have
> no self which is apart from the All, and this All includes
> change. Therefore, being one with the All, you are also
> one with change. Now from that viewpoint, peer deeply
> into change. Change takes place in our age or in human
> relations. How does that affect your real nature? In
> no way. Allness is merely adding variety to the way it
> expresses itself. Now look even deeper. You cannot be
> hurt because you yourself are not apart from the change,
> for you are change itself. And listen to this. Since you are
> the All, you allow change, you approve it, you are happy
> with it.

F. GOD IS ALL THAT IS REAL.

The hardest time to remember this is when great excitement is present over how well things seem to be going. I recall when I was training a new sales representative. On his first try he made a sale and was extremely excited. An alarm went off in my mind because I knew that if he got this excited when things went well, he would likely fall deeply on the other side when things did not go so well. This is what happened. The next day he didn't make a sale after several attempts and fell into dejection. He quit shortly afterwards.

Your Central Self is like a giant radio station that never ceases to broadcast its cheerful messages. This broadcast does not swing like a pendulum between excitement and depression; it is tranquil and constant. The next time you are in a mental spin, when the world is pressing in on you with either good or bad fortune, take a deep breath and say in your Heart, "God is all that is real."

G. WHAT DO I NEED TO REMEMBER?

A dazed and groggy world wants you to forget the higher facts you know so clearly. But all you need is a pause, an open space, to attract back to your awareness the rich and purpose-filled life you have in fact never lost.

For example, when you have a spare moment at a red light or while standing in line, pause and ask yourself, "What do I need to remember?" The most amazing and refreshing insights arrive at the least expected moments. You don't have to be on a high and isolated mountain somewhere to receive the highest revelations. They can arrive while you're walking to the mailbox!

PURPOSE TIP: In order to remember, the facts first had to be inside of you. They are there. You can remember.

"What do I need to remember?" activates your power of *listening*. The essence of spiritual growth is to *remember*. "He that hath ears to hear, let him hear" (Mark 4:9). You have heavenly ears, not primarily to hear something being told to you by someone else, but to listen and hear the content of your soul's still small voice (see 1 Kings 19:12).

SUMMARY OF VITAL SECRET #7

We can see the value of most religions in teaching the old-fashioned virtues of cleanliness, honesty and humility. We can also see how many religions tend to foster the concept of "God outside of you, apart from you, in a future heaven out there." As discussed in the Forgiveness section, at the core of the false self is the illusion of separation from God.

"The spirit down here in man and the spirit up there in the sun, in reality are only one spirit, and there is no other one" (The Upanishads). "I searched for God and found only myself. I searched for myself and found only God" (Sufi proverb).

As your requests grow more focused, a magnificent transition occurs in which you merge with the Source of help rather than identifying yourself with what needs healing. Eventually, even the "self" that is seeking enlightenment disappears in this supreme realization of your rich and purpose-filled life.

Either there is one mind and one Spirit, as the Bible and other sacred books teach, or there's not. To know your oneness with God is to truly honor God; it is to dissolve the petty little ego that has thrashed around for years trying to be its own god.

Ralph Waldo Emerson declares, "All spiritual being is in man. A wise old proverb says, 'God comes to see us without bell,' that is, as there is no screen or ceiling between our heads and the infinite heavens, so is there no bar or wall in the soul where man, the effect, ceases, and God, the cause, begins."

Q & A

Q: Where do I begin?

A: Let's turn again to that remarkable book by Mr. Howard, *Esoteric Encyclopedia of Eternal Knowledge*:

> Some of the regions along the Persian Gulf are among the driest on earth. There are no streams and rain seldom falls. Human life would be impossible in some of these areas except for a fortunate occurrence. One day some swimmers dived deep enough into the sea to make a startling and delightful discovery. Undersea springs poured huge quantities of fresh water upwards towards the surface.
>
> The swimmers obtained goatskin bags, dived through the layer of salt water and filled their bags with pure water. The life-giving water became available to all who knew the secret of the undersea springs.

Your Soul's reunion with God/Truth/Reality is a connection, not a petition. The most sacred things cannot be taught by human lips.

Q: How can we deepen the intensity of our requests?

A: Formulate a sincere intention, cherish it for a moment or two, then let it go to find its way inwardly to "the underground springs." The meaning of faith is the certainty that your prayer is heard, that a connection is made and the prayer finds its way home. Prayers for wisdom, awareness and honesty, directed to the Heart, are always answered, even though we may not be fully aware of the manifestation for some time to come.

Q: How can we know we're working in the right way? What can we watch for?

A: Watch your inner conditions throughout the coming day and try to detect rightness, trueness and goodness as it struggles to break through the darkness that surrounds and overwhelms it. You can see it. And the very act of seeing it a little more clearly each time you look increases the brilliance of that light while it's struggling to break free. You can cooperate with it by listening, by observing, by knowing that it is there. It will eventually free you of *all*, I said *all* suffering and confusion and self-deception so there will only be the Light, the Goodness, that is in charge of you.

PURPOSE TIP: Your task in life is to shift the Center of your life from the mental—the lower, to the spiritual—the higher. Your spiritual Center is permanent happiness.

HEART HINTS

1. When you say "Truth, please make everything clear to me," you can magnify the effectiveness of this request by taking pen and paper in hand, and letting your True Self write everything out for you.

2. When you request, "God, you give me the strength and I'll give you the credit," you open the door to more assistance than you may presently be able to handle, but dare to open the door anyway!

3. Difficult experiences are perfect opportunities to wake up in the middle of the storm and transform the Heart.

4. Society wants you on a roller coaster of thrills followed by dejection, so get off by daring to proclaim "God is all that is real" when things seem to be going well. It is then easier to "get off" when things do not seem to be going well.

5. Everything you need to remember is yours alread. Only a connection needs to be made and the request "What do I need to remember?" is it.

6. Your Central Self is a geyser of spiritual nutrition, and *NowFacts* awaken this vertical flow. "But whosoever drinketh of the water that I shall give him shall never thirst; but the water that I shall give him shall be in him a well of water springing up into everlasting life" (John 4:14).

7. *Listen* to your innermost self, the part of you yearning to be free. Dare to let it have its way.

8. When you send your requests to the inner geyser, you are asking truly; you are not "asking amiss" (James 4:3). What a relief to end the frustration of sending your prayers "out there somewhere."

9. When people think they must travel somewhere or find a teacher in order to win this wisdom, they have yet to understand that daily life *is* the advanced field of spiritual practice, the domain where life's most wonderful lessons bloom like springtime.

10. Here's a wonderful *NowFact* to conclude this discussion on Receptive Request: "God, let your will, your way, be my will, my way."

HOW TO MASTER *THE LANGUAGE*
OF AWAKENING

Once upon a time there was a man who decided to paint his barn. He went to the local hardware store to buy 30 gallons of paint. He returned the next day to buy 30 more. The day after that he returned and purchased more. Finally the curiosity of the store owner got the best of him and he drove out to see what in the world would need that much paint. He couldn't believe his eyes. His customer had stacked the cans of paint around the outside of the barn! In dismay he asked him, "May I ask you one simple question? Have you ever heard of the word *apply*?"

Growth with *NowFacts* proceeds in three stages:

A. Planting

B. Persistence

C. Mastery

A. PLANTING

Success with these principles depends on having a lack of concern over seeing results. The anxiety of trying to get somewhere, of trying to be enlightened, only strengthens the illusion of a separate self isolated from the whole of life.

Can you plant without concern over results? Yes. How? By knowing that the spirit behind *The Language of Awakening* does its own planting. It is the spirit itself employing memorization. It is not a separate you deciding to hunker down and memorize. It is a higher form of effort that harmonizes your wish to learn with the desire of the universe to unfold itself.

PURPOSE TIP: I can of mine own self do nothing
because I seek not mine own will, but the will of the
Father which hath sent me.

—*John 5:30*

For me to say that an indepth study of *The Language of Awakening* is right and necessary for you would be highly presumptuous. Perhaps it will be something that happens later. However, if it does resonate now, if you sense something of immense value in *The Language*, then I invite you to let the Spirit carry it through.

Here's a six-point summary of how to make the most of *The Language of Awakening*:

1. Choose two or three *NowFacts* that have an especially clear resonance for you. Write them on a card. Carry this card with you and work with these statements for a few days. Carry extra cards to record your insights and connections.

2. When you feel the time is right, move on to the next two or three *NowFacts*. There's no schedule or pace you have to match. *These are doorways, not destinations.*

3. Keep your collection of cards and occasionally take a day or two for a review.

4. Pay close attention to statements that stir up resistance. For example, Steve J. felt at first that "That is your _____ (fear, regret, worry), not mine" seemed uncaring. He applied it and discovered that the best way he could really help someone was

to maintain his independence and refuse to participate in their self-generated anguish. Steve observed, "This allows essence to speak to essence, which I've found is the most truly helpful thing I can give to another."

5. Develop your own concise statements. For example, David G. created this powerful statement to help with Vital Secret #3 (instant choice): "Where is my attention this moment?" David added, "This *NowFact* helps me realize when my thoughts have drifted to negative areas."

6. *NowFacts* begin as mental statements, but they hold so much intensity and power they don't stop there. You'll increasingly feel them resonate throughout your Being, whether they are used silently or audibly.

Rarely before has there been collected in one place such concise and spiritually effective tools. So read through *The Language of Awakening* a time or two, then return for more focused work. Employ the power of memorization and you'll be amazed how the *NowFacts* lift you.

HERE IS A WONDERFUL BONUS YOU RECEIVE FOR INVESTING IN THIS BOOK!

We've prepared a 3 × 5 card deck for you! You get all the *NowFacts* plus key ideas on how to apply them. Index cards make this system portable and can greatly enhance your learning. To download your free copy now send an email to:

lifecards@aweber.com

You'll need to pick up some 3 × 5 index card paper for your computer printer. It's easy to find at local office supply stores and online. Each 8 ½ × 11 sheet has three perforated index cards. The computer file we send you uses a special template so all the index cards print out perfectly.

Important: You'll need to *confirm* the first email you receive and the card deck will follow. If you don't receive a response shortly after you confirm, check your spam filter. With the Microsoft Word attachment to the email, it may get mistakenly routed to your spam box. Read the instructions in my email on how to open and print the file for best results.

There's no need to rush, but there is a tremendous need to focus. Let this planting be deep and thorough. *NowFacts*, when applied and skillfully used (which comes through practice), generate more energy than reading a thousand books!

B. PERSISTENCE

You'll need to regain your focus again and again. Keep going no matter what. Have no fear as inner storms and upheavals appear; they are positive signs you are on the right road. False beliefs must be disturbed in order to be dismissed. Real spiritual teachings speak openly and plainly about this stage so you'll know what to expect.

Picture yourself in a small boat struggling to get away from a deserted island. The crashing waves make your departure difficult. Finally, you make it over the last wave and into the open sea. Your sail catches its first gust of wind, then the gust quickly disappears. You paddle until the wind returns. Further out at sea the wind arrives more often and stays in your sail for longer periods of time. You make it to the sea lanes, and an ocean liner, your Central Self, spots you and picks you up.

> Come, you lost atoms, to your Center draw
> And be the eternal mirror you saw;
> Rays that have wander'd into Darkness wide
> Return and back your sun subside.
>
> —Farid ud-Din Attar in the Sufi
> classic *Conference of the Birds*

Persistence is a virtuous power already present within the Spirit of Life. We express persistence, we do not create it. While it is a fact that God/Truth/Reality does all the work, I must also work to adjust my viewpoint and polish my receiving mechanism to receive what is present.

> My Father worketh hitherto, and I work.
>
> —*John 5:17*

C. MASTERY

At first memorization requires effort, quite a bit of it. It's not an easy journey. Just pick things right back up if you get sidetracked. Return over and over and over again to this grand task the Spirit of Life has invited you to. If you do, nothing, absolutely nothing, can block you from uncovering your rich and purpose-filled life.

PURPOSE TIP: The wish for the higher life must
be nourished and cultivated, but the fact that
you have the wish guarantees your success.

Practice reveals an abundance of energy inside the *NowFacts* and it starts to flow. This energy stirs up more energy. You begin to feel yourself supported by vast currents of power. No more life of reluctance. No more holding yourself back. It's time to step forward and *be* who you really are.

THE HEALING POWER OF VOICE AWARENESS

There's another dimension to *The Language of Awakening*: Know you are talking as you are talking. Have the light of awareness active at the moment you are speaking. Hear your own voice with all its subtleties. It is an amazingly effective barometer of unseen psychological states.

Voice awareness creates a great reservoir of energy in back of your speech. Not only is your speech more relevant and effective, but it has a lively and more natural tone as well. This leads to all kinds of benefits and insights, including instant recognition when your speech is weak and wavering.

Listen to yourself talk. Presently, you may be able to only look back and see what you said. But the time will come when you can listen to yourself talk right in the middle of your conversations.

You will feel new and true excitement as you detect yourself saying dumb things at the very moment you say them!

Noticing your speech expands your powers of thought detection. This is one power active in two directions—outwardly to voice and body, inwardly to thoughts and emotions.

TWO MORE WAYS TO ENHANCE YOUR PRACTICE

1. Before falling asleep at night take a few minutes to scan your day. Recall your experiences with *NowFacts*. When were you more aware? When were you unaware and preoccupied? What missteps were made and how quickly did you recover? What principle or realization touched your emotions today? These insights are priceless. This exercise connects up all your learning and helps you sleep more restfully.

2. Discussing your inner work with others is sometimes not the thing to do, especially when you are first embarking on a new practice. At this early stage, as powerful insights are coming together, talking about your experiences can lead to a dissipation of energy. The effect may not be seen, however, until a few weeks later when you find your focus has slipped. So at the start, practice *The Language of Awakening* in secret. Later, sharing your insights in wise and appropriate settings can be nourishing. But let the seeds sprout first.

✼ GARDEN 3 ✼

SILENCE

Open Doorways to the Heart's Vitality

WE LIVE IN A top-heavy society that has enthroned the intellect as the hub of life. Though the intellect can know amazing things for life on the everyday level, and developing its abilities is a perfectly sensible thing to do, its domain is not spiritual reality. It needs a compassionate master— your awakened Heart!

When I was a child, Mrs. English's second grade class was an interesting place to be. Every day after lunch she turned out the light for the children to take a nap, then she departed for the teachers' lounge. An eager boy looked around the corner to make sure she was gone. The all-clear signal was given and the room erupted. Half an hour later Mrs. English returned. She stepped into the room and flicked the light switch twice, always twice. She did not have to say a word or raise a hand. Her presence effortlessly restored order.

PURPOSE TIP: Thinking too much is a symptom
of a dormant Heart. Instead of trying to push the
intellect into obedience, wake up your Central
Self. Thought then takes its rightful place and serves
your higher purposes, rather than obscure them.

WHAT ARE SILENT SESSIONS?

Silent Sessions are daily quiet time appointments with your Central
Self. You can sit quietly in a chair or on the floor, or lie comfortably on a couch or bed. I prefer a simple, solid chair with a touch
of padding where I can sit up comfortably, yet avoid the strain on
my knees that happens when I sit on the floor for extended periods of time.

Picture yourself waiting in your car at a train crossing. The train
rushes by so fast you cannot see the gap between the freight cars.
On another day you are at the same crossing but this time the train
moves more slowly. You can now look through the space between
the freight cars and see the beautiful scenery on the other side.

Silent sessions can be as brief as a few minutes in length. Having several pauses like this during your day can possibly have more
benefit than one longer session, though both have value. To say
"I'm going to meditate for 40 minutes every day" is a quite limiting viewpoint and way too elementary.

SEVEN TIPS FOR A SUCCESSFUL SILENT SESSION

Here are ways to get past the intellect's babble and into charming currents of quietness.

1. HAVE PEN AND PAPER CLOSE BY. When the mind thinks of things to be done, or comes up with creative ideas, write them down. Sometimes this is a defensive measure of the intellect to keep you out of silence; other times the ideas or insights are of higher quality. Either way, clear the slate. Get the ideas down and return to your task.

2. USE THE *NOWFACT*: "I AM HERE." A wonderful way to begin is to simply look around, be present, sense the room (or the outdoors) and feel yourself in it. Notice the colors, the plants, the furniture, the space. Let your attention move away from the concerns of the day and reconnect to the present moment.

3. BE AWARE OF YOUR BREATHING. Without trying to modify your breathing, simply notice it. If you detect tension, don't *try* to let it go, but simply stay with your awareness. Notice how awareness itself generates a release. The release happens naturally, effortlessly, on its own time table. A little practice with this proves the presence of an inherent internal release mechanism that lets go for us.

   Also, you don't have to close your eyes. We're not trying to imitate the yogis here. You can experiment and try it both ways eyes open, eyes closed. Open and relaxed eyes can often help quiet the mind.

4. MAKE THE TRANSITION TO LISTENING, TO QUIET

RECEPTIVITY. Watch how much easier it all becomes when you listen to the open spaces of silence, in place of trying to make the intellect quiet. Silence is living, flowing, interesting. It is not a static destination. View your entire being as a sensitive listening instrument, all tuned into one place. Rohit Mehta writes:

> The river keeps itself pure by virtue of its movement. Thus it is movement that is the cause of purification. The silent mind is a pure mind. Such a mind is not to be mistaken for a stagnant mind. In the silent mind there is a movement—it is not a movement *of* the mind, but a movement *in* the mind. The mind that receives the current of life without any indulgence or resistance is ever pure. In such a mind there is an uninterrupted flow of life. The mind does not seek to collect the waters of life—it allows the waters to flow on. It is this movement of life that indeed keeps the mind pure and uncorrupt. In fact, movement is the very essence of purification.

Instead of trying to make the intellect quiet, apply your listening faculty. *Hear something new instead of battling something false.* This simple switch makes all the difference.

PURPOSE TIP: "Be still, and know that I am God."
—*Psalms 46:10*

5. **LET YOUR ENERGY SETTLE INTO YOUR HEART AND CIRCULATE.** Just as a newly-formed galaxy gathers inward for greater power and intensity, so does your True Self attract more of what it already is. Our rich and purpose-filled life is found as we allow ourselves to be drawn toward our Center. Underground springs open and vitality flows vertically, entreating us to join levels of insight and understanding *that already exist*. This is the secret science of prayer taught in the Bible and other sacred books. Anthony de Mello writes:

> The Master became a legend in his lifetime. It was said that God once sought his advice: "I want to play a game of hide-and-seek with humankind. I've asked my Angels what the best place is to hide in. Some say the depth of the ocean. Others say the top of the highest mountain. Others still the far side of the moon or a distant star. What do you suggest?"
>
> Said the Master, "Hide in the human heart. That is the last place they will think of!"

PURPOSE TIP: Keep your attention on
the center point inside. It will expand.

Truth is like a giant castle—safe, secure and at peace. But we think we have to stand on the castle walls fighting all the surrounding enemies. Why don't we just realize the complete safety of the castle and join the magnificent feast served at center court? Silence is what the castle is all about.

6. LET YOUR SOUL SUCCEED. If need be, remind the intellect you'll tend to what it wants to think about later, but for now you're doing something else. Let all mental effort cease. Don't anticipate anything. Just see what happens. Dare to turn loose the full power of your Soul.

Robert Browning refers to "The Imprisoned Splendor" in his poem, "Paracelsus":

> Truth is within ourselves, it takes no rise
> From outward things; whate'er you may believe
> There is an inmost center in us all
> Where truth abides in fullness; and around,
> Wall upon wall, the gross flesh hems it in,
> This perfect, clear perception which is Truth.
> A baffling and perverting carnal mesh
> Binds it and makes all error; and to know
> Rather consists in opening out a way
> Whence the imprisoned splendor may escape
> Than in effecting entry for a light
> Supposed to be without.

As you increasingly refer to the "inmost center . . . where truth abides in fullness," you have a marvelous feeling of joy and release. Your overriding aim at this point is to open more doors and windows around the splendor, to let your Soul rise and be free.

PURPOSE TIP: "Can you give the wisdom of your heart
precedence over the learning of your head?"

—*Tao Te Ching*, Lao-Tzu

---

7. APPLY A DISPERSAL EXERCISE. When concluded with a quiet session, take a moment to disperse and circulate the energy. Rub your hands together quickly for 20 to 60 seconds or so. Notice how warm the hands can get! This shows that the energy generated in these sessions can be substantial. This is a "cool down" exercise—a Taoist technique. You can also rub your hands quickly down your arms and through the ends of your fingers, massage your face, stretch a little.

Spiritual health makes you healthy in every area. You will be physically healthier, you will rest well at night. Everything will be better as a result of spiritual health.

SUMMARY

The benefits of quiet time cannot be sought haphazardly. The only way to benefit is through consistency. Yes, the intellect will often be jumpy, sometimes very much so, but with relaxed and intelligent persistence everything comes together. Never judge the value of a quiet session by how quiet the mind is. Sometimes we gain the most value when we patiently persist in spite of the intellect's antics.

The silence of your Center is magnetic. It has built-in appeal. It seeks itself. Here is an illustration from my Vernon Howard class notes:

> There was once a country that had four kings. The kings lived far from each other. Communication was slow and the handling of the kingdom's affair was difficult.
>
> But over the years the kings moved closer and closer together. Eventually they decided to build a giant castle in the center of the kingdom. When the castle was completed, all the kings moved in. Now the kingdom was governed with perfect harmony.

As you continue to develop, your inner parts move closer together and eventually merge into one.

PURPOSE TIP: "A quiet mind without a quiet Heart is impossible."
—*Dr. Chapin*

PURPOSE TIP: "When you ask, 'Who am I?' and there is silence, could it be that the silence you hear is the answer?"
—*Vernon Howard*

❧ GARDEN 4 ❧

REST AND RECREATION

THE SPIRITUAL QUEST IS not a race to win. Nothing can be forced. It is a wonderful relief to know that a game of tennis, or a day in the park with the children, or a mystery novel, music, or whatever you enjoy, takes you to the Garden of Rest and Recreation—a place with the sole purpose of furthering your growth and development.

We need to guard against picking up false ideas along the way of what it means to be "spiritual." In attempting to give up old thinking patterns, we can mistakenly lead ourselves to renounce activities we naturally enjoy, believing we're doing a good thing. Though some activities are not conducive to our higher aims and must be relinquished, others are fun, harmless and invigorating. We'll still have our individual preferences for certain fun-filled activities, and others will have theirs.

When you live with spiritual nobility, then you can have the lunch, you can watch the TV show, you can watch the baseball game, you can work out in your garden, you can play the piano and do anything you want to do that's legitimate, that's relaxation from hard mental or physical work. All your centers must be exercised, which is why entertainment and amusement are valid and necessary.

The more we apply ourselves in Gardens 1, 2 and 3, the more deeply we find ourselves enjoying the rich and healthy rewards Garden 4 offers us. The wise are playful, which nourishes their intensity.

❧ SECTION THREE ❧

THE POWER OF
VERTICAL THINKING

THE SELF-IMPRISONED BIRD

SEVERAL YEARS AGO MY wife and I were in Colorado for a speaking engagement. We had an afternoon free and visited the local zoo, sauntering back to the exotic bird section. There we saw a circular fence, probably 18 feet high and some 60 feet across. It was very odd to us that the fence had no top to it.

We observed a rare bird over in a far corner. I reasoned that the keepers must have clipped its wings so it could not fly away. Then suddenly the bird went into full flight to a tree on the other side of the cage. Obviously I was wrong. The bird's wings were fine.

I found a zoo attendant and asked him why the bird didn't fly away. "The reason is very simple," he said. "This bird was raised in captivity. When it was young it was placed in a cage with a top on it. Every time it tried to fly away it would hit the ceiling. Now, the bird never tries to escape. It is convinced the top of the cage is still there."

"How strange," I thought, "and what a perfect example of a 'life of reluctance.' The bird has the energy for flight, but it's directed into maintaining false walls. The misdirected energy causes every limit he experiences."

The answer is never to try and create more energy as we already have a remarkable abundance. The answer is to *reclaim the energy* invested in illusionary walls, and let it rejoin the vertical current flowing from the depths of your Being.

HORIZONTAL THINKING

Horizontal thinking is the self-created mental cage where one looks out and *sees* all kinds of obstacles. It envisions problems being solved "tomorrow" when more wisdom is collected, a mentor is found or circumstances change. It likes to play things "safe" by staying in suggested and approved channels. Hope for a better tomorrow is its faulty compass.

Horizontal thinking is a misuse of the mind because it projects the attainment of happiness into the future. Religious empires, for example, are built on this "happiness tomorrow" mind-set—"Heaven in the afterlife" or "Power will appear when you reach level 9."

When we plan to be happy tomorrow, we are thinking horizontally, whether through the eventual attainment of financial success, religious rewards, the acquisition of a new home or car or the entrance or exit of someone in our life. This type of thinking can be compared to the greyhound races where the dogs chase an imaginary rabbit around the racetrack. They never catch it. Likewise, when we chase happiness with horizontal thinking, it proves to be elusive.

EXAMPLES OF HORIZONTAL THINKING

A classic example of horizontal thinking occurred centuries ago when a few brave souls dared to believe that the earth was round and revolved around the sun. Religious empires and governments were built on the premise that the earth was the center of the universe and all the heavens circled it.

When it was proved that the world was round (and not the center of the universe), the response from the religious and scientific authorities of the day was to get rid of the people who spread such heresies. New ideas never fit well in old thought structures. "Neither do men put new wine in old bottles, else the bottles break" (Matthew 9:17).

Alexander Graham Bell strived for many years to get his telephone accepted for commercial use. The Wright brothers searched for years to find funding for their airplane. Kodak turned away a new photographic process because "they saw no value in it." That new process was later taken to the market by a company named Xerox.

In the 1960s the Swiss manufactured 65 percent of the watches sold on earth—mechanical constructions with gears and springs. Someone invented an electronic watch, but the Swiss watchmakers saw it as nothing more than a trivial item of little interest. Japan, however, saw the electronic watch as a gold mine and made a whole new industry from it. By 1980 they had reduced the Swiss market share to about 20 percent. (Examples are from Joel Barker's book, *Paradigms: The Business of Discovering the Future.*)

Another great example is the life of Christ. The principles

Christ taught stirred extreme hatred and hostility among his con-
temporaries. They felt threatened, which is the classic response to
radically new information from those who have a vested interest in
the maintenance of the established viewpoint because their power
and security flows from its continuance.

Horizontal thinking claims the treasures we seek may some-
day exist for us; we don't have them now, but we may in the future.
Vertical thinking says that the treasures we seek are already present.
We don't have to manufacture them, "positive think" them or "visualize" them into existence. The awakening of your Heart releases a
vertical flow and lifts your awareness to treasures that already exist.
Location is possession!

Does this mean we neglect to plan our business and family
affairs? Of course not. We plan and think clearly and efficiently.
But because we're *vertical* in our thinking, we know that our happiness is not dependent on the outcome of our plans. We are happy
before the plans are made, while making the plans and after the
plans play out to either success or failure. We do all we can to make
the plans successful, but our identity is not wrapped around out-
comes. Many of the richest opportunities for wisdom and healing
occur when things do not work out as we had planned. We can
watch for reactions and disappointments and if they appear, we can
work profitably through a previously unseen layer of the false self.

Vertical thinking also makes possible the practice of forgiveness and instant recovery. When we make a mistake by slipping
back to horizontal thinking, we can return immediately to vertical thinking the moment we see our misstep. Freedom exists now,
this instant, in the vertical direction. It is like the old Tarzan mov-

ies where there is *always* a vine for the hero to reach up and catch. There is always a principle available that lifts us above any form of criticism. The answer is to move vertically by absorbing the lessons immediately at hand as our day unfolds. *The Language of Awakening* provides focus for doing so.

Here's an extremely important fact: You do not have to improve the swamp. You do not have to fight negativity. You do not have to change it or modify it in any way. There's a clearly marked path leading right out of the swamp and up the side of a beautiful mountain. Ignore the howls of protest from the "swamp improvement committee" when you leave them alone with the problems they cherish, and begin your vertical ascent.

Horizontal thinking leads people to believe that with just a little more time, a little more effort and the use of the right method, they will be able to clear the swamp once and for all and finally live in peace. Vertical thinking perceives that your rich and purpose-filled life is present now, fully developed, existing on a higher level that we can immediately approach. Even one inch of movement in the vertical direction produces a contrast that can be instantly felt. We begin to remember what we already know.

PURPOSE TIP: There is a high state of development where you receive the gifts already created. Spiritual growth is the ascendance into higher and higher feelings—*spiritual* feelings.

HORIZONTAL THINKING AND RESISTANCE

The horizontal thinking paradigm attacks vertical ideas. It often calls vertical ideas negative. Sensing a great threat, it seeks to steer you away from them without delay. This is why anyone who sincerely works to apply vertical principles experiences resistance. We feel new power one day and heaviness the next and wonder what's going on.

The higher you go, two things happen with increasing intensity. On one hand, you feel bright and alive, cheerful and refreshed; on the other hand, you feel heaviness and confusion. These states alternate back and forth. Light is breaking through new layers of darkness. The process you are going through is perfectly safe and secure. Allow time for a novel or movie, tennis or golf, or whatever you enjoy doing for entertainment (Garden #4). Balance is the key. Unfoldment cannot be rushed or forced.

The resistance inside the horizontal patterns towards the appearance of vertical ideas is the resistance of the false patterns. Be aware of how the patterns want you to think it is *your* resistance so you will side with them. Everyone encounters these obstacles and those who persist and stay aware exit with smiles.

THE SPIRAL STAIRCASE

One of the best analogies for vertical thinking is the spiral staircase. We must confront things we thought we already resolved. However, as we ascend we meet these issues on a slightly higher level of insight than before. Our perception is cleansed and we discern connections not previously seen.

We're often invited to explore something we thought we long

ago left behind. It is a huge relief to know that the reappearance of anything negative does not mean we've failed or fallen, but simply that we're ready now to free a new slice of the originally pure energy inside the negative pattern.

Consider that only 66 years passed from Kitty Hawk to Apollo 11's lunar landing! Things happened quickly once the fundamental laws of flight were discerned and applied. Likewise, the unfolding of your Heart occurs swiftly once you recognize its supreme value and harmonize with its wise and compassionate content.

HORIZONTAL THINKING VS. VERTICAL THINKING

Here are three examples of the differences between these two types of thinking:

ONE:

Horizontal thinking: I must fight to be free.
Vertical thinking: I must let go to be free.

The swamp is a gigantic rope-tossing machine. Its "success" depends on one thing, you catching the ropes. Wisdom seekers often make the mistake of catching the ropes, then fighting and struggling to be free. What we can do is discover where we're holding on, then let go! Gradually our awareness increases and we're able to detect the ropes approaching and refuse them.

Watch as the rope tossers change their tactics. First they approach with ropes of flattery, gossip and special group inclusion. If that doesn't work, they'll toss ropes of intimidation, guilt and threats of exclusion. They'll try every trick in the book to turn you away from your rich and purpose-filled life.

As you practice refusing the ropes, you find with great delight that the same principle applies to inner negativities. You'll see thought ropes of anger, worry, guilt and other similar emotions tossed within your own mind, and you'll wisely choose to leave them alone. Here is beautiful synergy between Key #3 (instant choice) and #4 (independence and empathy). By choosing to *refuse* the ropes we nourish our independence.

TWO:

> *Horizontal thinking:*   I need to escape the pain.
> *Vertical thinking:*   I release the pure energy present in the pain.

Lingering problems, such as worry, frustration and tension are not enemies to battle but false patterns that house originally pure energy. These patterns are dissolved by uncovering them and consciously inhabiting them—by reconnecting to the pure energy and reminding it of a higher flow, thus setting it free!

The sure sign of a successful exploration of a false pattern is that the problem temporarily intensifies. What is really happening is that you are now seeing the roots of the pattern, instead of just suffering on the surface. This is why solving any problem, even on the everyday level at home or office, always includes a healthy upheaval at the beginning. Problems are dissolved by allowing them to intensify, with awareness, and not by trying to control or avoid them or push them into a smaller place.

Spiritual success requires a willingness to face our inner world as it is, and not as we imagine it. J. Krishnamurti notes, "The pure act of seeing the fact, whatever the fact be, brings its own understanding and from this, mutation takes place."

Synergy is wonderfully present between Key #2 (self-observation) and #6 (efficiency). It is highly efficient to observe the mind and release the energy temporarily encased in false patterns, just as the health science of acupuncture seeks to remove blockages and restore health by increasing the flow of life energy.

THREE:

Horizontal thinking: I will think positive thoughts.

Vertical thinking: I will discover the wise and cheerful thoughts in my Heart and learn to express them.

Positive thinking and its endless offshoots tends to be a popular philosophy. It attracts many to its ranks because it appears at first to be true. Here's an illustration of the crucial, pivotal difference between inner development and positive thinking:

Two men were on a long journey covering the same rough terrain. The first man started quickly but began to fade and stumble. The second man started slowly but kept going at a consistent pace.

A small group of wise men were watching both of the travelers. They wanted to discern their thinking. So they asked the one who faltered and stumbled, "What is your underlying philosophy in regards to this journey?" The man replied, "I am determined to be stronger than this terrain!" That's interesting, the wise men said among themselves. That sounds positive.

Then they asked the other man, "What is your underlying philosophy in regards to this journey? How do you approach it in your thinking?" The second man replied, "I am working to discover a power stronger than this terrain."

Those involved in positive thinking may appear to leap ahead right out of the gate. Later on, however, the strength their philosophy seems to possess starts to fade. Why? Because positive thinking is personality based, not Heart based; it is mental, not spiritual. The consistant man, on the other hand, sought to harmonize with sources of vitality already present. He sought to *discover*, not to create.

THE VALUE OF SELF-IMPROVEMENT

Though positive thinking as a philosophy has huge underlying flaws, self-improvement is important and legitimate. Let's not confuse the two.

PURPOSE TIP: "An orderly mind is a powerful instrument."
—Vernon Howard

For example, over the last several years I've studied the Alexander Technique. It is widely used by musicians, actors and other performing artists, including public speakers. The Alexander Technique reawakens our capacity to move with less tension and more ease and grace. Using simple everyday tasks, like getting out of a chair, the student of the technique learns to let go of the end (in this case being out of the chair) and be aware the entire way there. Yet, the Alexander Technique is self-improvement. It helps serve the purpose of an orderly mind, but it is not spirituality.

Picture a helicopter that lands on top of a tall building. The helicopter symbolizes spirituality. It lifts you up and away to lofty mountains.

We can associate the building with self-improvement. Yes, it does have a top. It is limited. However, the building is crucial to us for the simple reason that the helicopter doesn't descend down to the streets!

There are valuable things to explore in the self-improvement arena! For example, consider music, history, dance, theatre, painting and mathematics. How about journaling, comunication techniques, efficiency, finances and health? A major area of self-improvement are the old-fashioned virtues. Mr. Howard loved the old-fashioned virtues of honesty, cleanliness, thrift and responsibility and often referred to them in his talks.

Illustration: A father once had a fabulous collection of rare and valuable books. He wanted to give them to his son. So the father carefully boxed them up and transported them to his son's house. However, his son had not prepared a place to receive the books. His house was cluttered and dusty. The father told him, "When you prepare a proper place to receive the books, you can have them." The son went to work and built beautiful, dust proof bookcases. When they were completed, the father cheerfully delivered the books.

Like the 4th Garden of Rest and Recreation, we have our natural inclinations and favorite areas for self-improvement endeavors. Taste the possibilities and find what's right for you.

HEART HINTS:

1. Like the bird raised in captivity, we were influenced by people when we were young who transferred to us their love of low vibrations—their horizontal mind-set. Through vertical thinking we can transcend these influences forever.

2. Horizontal thinking believes happiness will arrive when things change. Vertical thinking peceives that happiness is *now* and the mind's present location must change.

3. Your awakened Heart generates immense energy that lifts your perception to currents of wisdom eager to instruct you.

4. The horizontal thinking paradigm inevitably labels vertical thinkers as deserters. When you hear the complaint, "You used to be so nice," you can rest assured you are making real progress.

5. It is a great relief to comprehend that vertical thinking is on a spiral. You will meet things you thought you left behind, perhaps years ago. However, you meet them on a new level with possibilities to learn much more.

6. Remember the powerful mental picture of the rope tossers. Refuse to catch the ropes! This can be used with great effectiveness in both daily life and in observing the operations of the mind.

7. The universe is energy. Sometimes this energy gets pulled in to false patterns, so our work is not to battle the pattern but to work our way through it and touch the pure energy. Your touch (your awareness) sets the energy free.

8. Positive thinking is perhaps the second or third story in a 50-story building of self-improvement studies. There are far more valuable things to study that can help develop an orderly mind, which is the real aim of self-improvement.

9. Christ said things with such beautiful brevity as in "Friend, go up higher" (Luke 14:10). Instead of struggling with the intellect to understand, awaken the vertical currents of your Central Self and you'll be lifted to where your rich and purpose-filled life already exists.

THE SUPERWISDOM
DICTIONARY

40 Key Words for Contemplation
and Transformation

THIS DICTIONARY IS A treasury of focused facts. It was 15 months in the making, written over my kitchen table as several old-time friends met often and discussed and challenged each other on what the words really meant.

One good way to profit from this dictionary is to use mind maps. Much good information is on the internet; just search "mind maps." Place the word in a circle in the center of the page, then make your connections in spokes radiating from the center. The highest value arrives as you throw your own logs on the fire. What are *your* connections and insights?

PURPOSE TIP: "Remember, anything that has not been
discovered by your own intelligent effort has not
been discovered at all."

—Vernon Howard

ASLEEP: A dull state in which the mind is disconnected from
the present moment. When asleep, one does things without
really knowing he or she is doing them. For example, he places
his car keys somewhere but doesn't remember where, passes
the desired exit while driving his automobile and has to turn
around or walks into a room and forgets why he went there.
When asleep, one says things he or she later regrets because
awareness was not present to halt the mouth. This disconnect
spawns a thousand problems that awakening heals. *Synonyms:*
preoccupied, unaware.

AWAKENING: Begins with honest self-questioning. For example,
"Is this all there is to life?" Awakening dawns in the open spaces
following these intense questions—not from frantic efforts to
locate the answers. There are several key stages to awakening
including: 1) detecting how lost and unhappy almost everyone
is, including the "leaders," without getting a sense of superiority yourself; 2) seeing the futility and emptiness of your present
ways of thinking and acting, without despair; 3) perceiving ever
new depths to truths and principles you once thought you fully
comprehended, without egotism and its pride of accomplish-
ment; 4) receiving influxes of light and good cheer that increase
in intensity, without trying to recreate them; and 5) experiencing upheavals and protests from the false self as the influx of
light and good cheer intensifies, without self-condemnation.

Awakening is unending learning, unfolding and ever-deep-
ening oneness with God/Truth/Reality. It *is* the rich life.

AWARENESS: Vernon Howard defines awareness as having the
mind present with the body during the activities of daily life.
Awareness is unity with the present moment. It begins as a tiny

seed pulsating with the wish to expand. It brings together spirit, mind, emotions and body under one flag. The New Testament compares it to the mustard seed, small in the beginning but eventually the largest of trees. Awareness is inherently expansive. It "grows itself" when granted the opportunity. It is dynamic and constantly probes the edge.

CENTER: The kingdom of heaven within the great oasis. Also, "the stone which the builders rejected" (Mark 12:10) as they constructed the intellect's "tower of Babel" (Genesis 11). The source of breath, silence, voice, wisdom and vitality known by the ancients, but long dismissed and forgotten by our top-heavy society. *Synonyms:* heart, *hara* (Japanese), essence, belly (New Testament, John 7:38 King James Version), *dan-tien* (Chinese).

CLEAR MIND: A clear mind has great power for focus and appropriate action. It quickly returns to its home, the present moment, when the need for thinking and action conclude. A clear mind gets the facts and easily says yes or no. If it is unsure, it seeks more information; it does not battle its uncertainty. A clear mind naturally disdains clutter and inefficiency. It enjoys new projects and challenges. Its energies are never squandered in the mental churning of regrets, fears and worries, as with the unclear. *Synonyms:* order, cleanliness.

DARKNESS: Darkness restricts; it tries to squeeze you into a smaller space. Light, on the other hand, releases you to a constantly expanding space. The core of darkness is insecurity, which explains why it is so controlling and oppressive. Darkness struggles to confirm itself but can never successfully do so. It runs in packs; darkness can never stand alone. It also has very clever recruiting techniques; for example, trying to get you to think toward someone in the same way it does. It is cunning, but not intelligent. *Synonyms:* insecurity, oppression, self-condemnation, slander, cowardness.

EGOTISM: Formed in darkness as the individual accepts the lie that he or she has an isolated self in opposition to life's natural currents of change.

Unfortunately, but predictably, egotism likes to get involved in "spiritual pursuits" and prove how much it knows. It can write captivating books and give stirring talks. Only light in one's self can detect "spiritual" egotism.

ENERGY: Life's unified field of power. It is the same power that raises your hand *and* whirls Mars through space. Energy is pure in its original form, but distorted by slumbering minds and diverted to the maintenance of a false self.

You have a choice as to how you deploy your energy. You can use it to build a spiritual empire or you can let darkness use your energy to further its influence. Since energy cannot be hoarded, *how* you use it is the single most important choice you make.

ESOTERIC: The esoteric is hidden only by the public's inability to perceive its value. It is available to all but chosen by few.

Esotericism is about self-reliance and digging your own well for spiritual refreshment. Esotericism produces men and women who live a rich life and purpose-filled life by firsthand experience. Esotericism is *internal meaning*, not structure or labels. It proves this by constant adaptation over the centuries to place and culture. Rigid minds hold on to visible forms, but the esoteric is the *eternal purpose* at the core of it all.

EVIL: "There are two types, active evil and passive evil" (Vernon Howard). Active evil is aggressive. It attempts to prevent the truth from reaching people, whether in a truthful teaching, a really good book or a meaningful movie. It has many refined methods, including ignoring the truly beneficial by highlighting inferior alternatives in its place. It tries to chip away at decency and your sensing of the beautiful, including art and music. Truth makes people self-reliant and perceptive which can lessen active evil's profit and influence.

Passive evil is being unaware and thus contributing by default to the perpetuation of the world's dark cloud. The only way to counter evil is to put it entirely out of business within oneself through the Heart's awakening.

Here is another extremely valuable contribution from Mr. Howard about evil. "Evil is a parasite. It only lives because you give it life. Withdraw your belief in it and it has nothing."

EXPERTHOOD: This coined word warns of what can happen to speakers and writers who take themselves too seriously. A huge trap on the spiritual path is the "advanced student"—one who merits attention and respect. Experthood is like walking up a high mountain, and 100 yards up catching a 100 pound boulder, then trying to carry it with you. "Spiritual experts" are heavy; they lose their sense of humor and the crucial ability to laugh at themselves. There is great happiness as one gives up trying to be "spiritual" and just decides to be *real*.

FALSE SELF: A hodgepodge collection of erroneous beliefs—a vapor entity that acts in your name. To "exist," the false self tries to attach to as many parts of you as possible, including nerves and muscles so it can "enjoy" its tension. The false self seeks to usurp the mind's natural ability to create mental pictures so it can use the energy to produce negative film clips. It throws ropes out to others in a desperate attempt to solidify the vapor with either an acceptance or a rejection. Its desperate cry is: "Whatever you do, just don't ignore me or I'll fade away."

As you realize your oneness with Life the vapor disintegrates. It poses intense objections so don't be discouraged. As the false self disappears amidst its own dire predictions of doom, if you continue to the Heart, *you* come alive with flowing good cheer.

FALSE SPIRITUAL TEACHER: False teachers are adept at mixing lies with truth, yet they are usually unaware it's happening. Some are skilled at the "tough and strong act" and their followers fall for it. Most have dynamic and attractive personalities. Others may claim a mantle of authority passed on to them by someone else. A false teacher can have lots of knowledge, having perhaps been in contact with a source of authentic teaching at one time; however, they chose to retain the core of the false self and use the knowledge for clever personal gain.

False teachers are threatened by a real source of spirituality and will not hesitate to try and influence one's thinking to keep them away from it, or at least diminish its importance. False teachers crave false followers. They collect people like a pawnshop owner collects merchandise to sell.

GOD/TRUTH/REALITY: It could be a bad sign if your author did not pause here in some doubt whether the word could be defined. Let's try for the fun of it.

The original source of all energy that is in direct communication with your spark of unfolding understanding.

148

Picture a football stadium lit up brilliantly at night. You walk into the center of the stadium holding a lighted candle. The vast light in the stadium and the light from your candle is *all one light.*

God/Truth/Reality teaches the candle that the silly half-time show on the field of the stadium was a temporary appearance and never touched the purity of the light. All is well! Who you *really* are has never left home.

HEART: The highly intelligent domain of emotional vitality that feels what it knows. So vital a principle it is used in the Bible 895 times.

HELL: 1) A state of inner anguish of trying to prove you are right when you are actually wrong; 2) believing the false self is you, and believing the mistakes of the false self have anything to do with you; 3) painful demands that others behave on a higher level than they are capable of behaving; 4) caving in to modern society's worst problem, which is *frantic stressful speed.*

INNER DEVELOPMENT: 1) an increasing ability to act on what you already know; 2) a deepening appreciation of silence; 3) the expanding understanding that God/Truth/Reality is behind all growth and you don't have to strain to make yourself grow; you need only harmonize with universal principles and *this* creates inner development—like a child who begins his study of mathematics and decades later does the mathematical equations to land a spaceship on a distant planet.

INSIGHT: Seeing something new about yourself or life. It is usually a sudden and energizing connection. Insights include perceiving both the false as false, and the true as true. They are always filled with light though often it is the light illuminating a falsehood and exposing it for what it is. *Synonyms:* connection, flash, opening.

INSTANT RECOVERY: The dropping of all self-condemnation following a mistake and the immediate realization that *now is new.* The practice of instant recovery develops your ability to learn the lesson quickly. Instant recovery is self-forgiveness as you let go of grudges against yourself for having acted in your sleep. Instant recovery and self-honesty were Mr. Howard's most frequent classroom themes.

INTELLIGENCE: The power that makes connections and understands how to develop. Intelligence knows how to handle every situation, which sometimes means a "yes" and sometimes a "no." Intelligence acts with tact and appropriate behavior. It also manifests good manners and is skilled in all forms of relationships, under all circumstances.

Intelligence is both firm and uncompromising with the appearance of falsehood, yet gentle and encouraging to the parts of you seeking what's true.

INTUITION: The quiet knowing that senses the best course, which sometimes means having the wisdom to do nothing. Taking pen and paper and considering your options blends intuition with mental clarity for better decisions.

JOLT: An unexpected experience that suddenly makes you aware of yourself. A jolt moves you out of familiar patterns into a new experience. Jolts are crucial for inner development. We must also learn to give them to ourselves, which *The Language of Awakening* reveals how to do. Also remember that false teachers love to give jolts, but because they come from a false place they produce only harmful results.

KINESTHETIC: A fascinating study of the connection between thought and muscle. Every thought produces a corresponding muscular connection, and every muscular pattern of movement and posture have an impact on one's outlook and attitudes. Wrong posture feels right because it is so familiar, and right posture at first feels wrong. A tense person usually doesn't know that he is.

LIFE-SUCCESS: Vernon Howard defined it with utmost brevity in his book *Psycho-Pictography: The New Way to Use the Miracle Power of Your Mind*: "You are a success when you *enjoy* your life." This enjoyment is our natural state; however, false doctrines, promoted by those in the desert with water to sell, have caused us to wander away from our inner oasis. You are not only a collection point for all cosmic power; you are that which you think you must obtain. *Synonyms:* rich life, purpose-filled life.

LOVE: The cool breeze flowing through the present moment. The inner circulation of cheerfulness arriving at unexpected moments. The understanding that what is real in you is never separate from what is real in someone else, but is one and the same. Love is untouched by competition and comparison because it knows when someone else grows, *you* grow. What is real in you blends *knowingly* with what is real in the universe.

MEDITATION: This word has so many possible meanings and connotations that its use can be confusing, which is why Mr. Howard avoided it. However, he was a strong proponent of quiet time of sitting or lying down and observing the mind with the intent to understand, not fight. Authentic silence can never be forced, but dawns in the space between two thoughts.

Meditation should never be separated from daily life. Practicing present moment awareness *is* meditation. Both quiet time *and* daily awareness constitute meditation. It's like two hands working in harmony.

MENTAL MOVIES: The unaware mind's tendency to run random film clips that trigger associations and negative emotions. Mental movies are a movement away from the present moment. Growth brings the power and skill to interrupt these useless film clips, and gently return to the vitality of the present moment.

MIND: With a small "m," mind refers to the faculty with the potential to operate with proficiency in daily life. A clear and well-operating mind is an asset in the spiritual quest, but only the spirit can release your rich and purpose-filled life dwelling in your Heart.

NEGATIVITY: Negativity has no basis or purpose in reality and can only "stay around" through the illegal use of originally pure energy. These patterns are not dissolved by opposition or denial, as with futile attempts at "positive thinking." They dissolve through diligent self-observation that consciously inhabits the patterns in order to thoroughly understand them. This gentle awareness reveals all their subtle nuances, without condemnation, thus freeing the energy.

PAUSE: 1) The wish for intelligence instead of the rush to being right; 2) A willingness to *not know* what to do; 3) A state of suspension that creates a space between stimulus and response; 4) A sudden and healthy release of muscular tension; 5) The quiet gap where everything is possible.

PERSISTENCE: A vital virtue that refuses to get discouraged when expanding light stirs up and exposes previously unseen areas of inner darkness. "Endure unto the end," as Christ instructs in

Mark 13:3. To the end of what? To the end of a false self that has dreamed its isolated existence apart from reality. "He that loseth his life . . . shall find it" (Matthew 10:39).

"If you have even a flicker of light you have cause for feeling fine. Be loyal to it. After awhile the flickering light turns to a steady glow" (Vernon Howard).

PRACTICAL THOUGHT: Thoughts serving useful purposes, as when planning an evening or learning a new profession. Negative thoughts are impractical. They waste energy. A truly spiritual person alternates all day long between practical thoughts and a state of higher awareness.

PRAYER: 1) As used in this book, a special technique that voices words in the Heart in order to stir dormant powers. The Bible also uses this meaning when it refers to "conversation in heaven." 2) Requests for invisible spiritual treasures, like insight and healing, directed to a source higher than the intellect. These requests are instantly granted by your True Self.

PURE PERCEPTION: Insight into yourself, another, a situation or event, *as it is*, without adding an ounce of self-righteous or critical spirit to what you see.

Pure perception sees another person as he or she is *now*, without limiting associations and references to past mistakes. This pure perception grants the opportunity to be new *this instant*. When you grant this opportunity to others, you strengthen your power to grant it to yourself.

PURPOSE: If you resolve to make union with God/Truth/Reality, the fundamental aim in life, you'll find that everything is transformed to serve this direction. For example, drinking a cup of tea or coffee with awareness satisfies both taste buds *and* spirit.

Driving with awareness to go shopping, then shopping with awareness, nourishes your Heart. With clarity of your fundamental purpose you have clarity in your secondary purposes; for example, your family, work and relationships. Everything clarifies as you grow from within. Therefore, "Seek ye first the kingdom of God, and all these things shall be added unto you" (Matthew 6:33).

REAL SPIRITUAL TEACHINGS: Focus is on quality of interest and never the quantity of people. Real spiritual teachings describe human nature as it is so it can be transcended. They do not flatter people with how "advanced" and "loving" they are. Because there's never a membership drive, they can be, and are, brilliantly honest and direct.

Real spiritual teachings place primary importance on individual transformation, not on the personality of a given writer or speaker. They include a natural and relaxed alternation between exposing darkness and hypocrisy on one hand, and revealing facts about the brightness of the awakened life on the other. Real spiritual teachings are practical and sensible; however, they are never part of a mass movement because "great truths do not take hold of the masses" (Chaung-tse).

SELF-COMMAND: Picture your hand reaching up to turn on a film projector. With increasing awareness you stop your hand before it reaches the projector button. Self-command dawns through unity with the present moment. You find yourself able to pause before acting, or before launching a mental movie. Self-command is the Heart awake and in charge of the mind.

SELF-HONESTY: A willingness to view your mind as it presently operates. Self-honesty is a willingness to see a misstep as a misstep. Self-honesty never contains self-condemnation. It is rigorous and demanding, yet forgiving and kind.

SHARKS: People who have refused their opportunity for spiritual development so often they have hardened. Sharks want others to join them in their misery. They are experts at every trick in the book including guilt, flattery, trickery and treacherous long-term planning. Sharks are drawn to spheres of influence like politics, education, government and religions. Other times, however, they resolve to bite the life out of just one or two people, perhaps family members. Because sharks are insecure they seek power over others in a futile attempt to satisfy their voracious appetite. To cease being a shark a shark would first have to see that he or she is a shark, and how many are going to do that? "The philosophy of society can be very simply stated. *Hit and get hit*" (Vernon Howard).

SPIRITUAL: The invisible dimension of life that flows through the present moment with meaning and purpose. The appearance or disappearance of a physical body has no impact on this sacred domain. Just as Niagara Falls continues to flow as bodies "come and go," so does the spiritual domain flourish without reference to human intervention.

SPIRITUAL MEMORY: A place in your Center where all insights of truth are recorded, connected and increasingly available as you develop.

SPIRITUAL PRACTICE: Gentle and inquisitive experimentation for the purpose of opening your perception to treasures already present.

STATUEHOOD: Truth is discovered through direct realization. It is in what the true teachers point to, and not their image or personality. This is very important, because if we identify too strongly with a teacher, something inside hardens, creating a huge obstacle to development. High and healthy respect for a true teacher never includes worship or fanaticism; these symptoms indicate a severe misunderstanding posing as sincerity and loyalty.

TRANSFORMATION: This is perfectly illustrated in nature when the butterfly emerges from the caterpillar. There is not just one transformation on the spiritual journey but many, as one leaves the old level without having the new, and then inhabits the new level without a trace of the old. A big step up is often proceeded by upheaval of some kind. Things fall apart, people leave, it all looks bleak. Then, the sun.

TRUE TEACHER: Those who have no compulsion to teach, yet when they do, it is obvious they practice what they teach. This congruence leads to ever higher levels of comprehension where there is no division between word and deed. Many can write or speak the truth while manifesting conduct that is diametrically opposed. The Source that inspired Christ and Buddha is the same Source from which a true teacher lives, and increasingly so.

TRUE SELF: The part of you that is one with God/Truth/Reality. Though your True Self may presently appear to be only 1 percent of you, that 1 percent is 100 percent pure and connected to the Supreme Source. So you are in a very good position. The energy of the entire universe is behind 1 percent growing to 2, and 2 percent growing to 3 and so on.

UNDERSTANDING: The breakthrough after a challenge where

spiritual principles were earnestly applied. Can be compared to actually tasting a peach, instead of just reading a description of a peach.

WISDOM: 1) The efficient and orderly use of energy; 2) Spaces of light existing between event and reaction; 3) A cheerful, open Heart that is flowing and beautiful. The understanding that, as Dr. Chapin said, "Here everything is perfectly all right and could not possibly be otherwise."

A GRAND SUMMARY OF THE
GREATEST OF ALL JOURNEYS

1. At the start we sense a vague call to something higher than the involvements and rewards of this world, but we're too close to the nonsense. Eventually something breaks open. For some of us it happens when we hit rock bottom or have a shocking experience. The inner pain reaches a certain point and we know we must find the Truth or perish.

2. We search for answers. We read many books and investigate various teachings. We keep looking, often in spite of great discouragement. Eventually we find the vein of pure gold that has existed throughout time.

3. With the experience of authentic gold (accurate inner development information), it is increasingly easier to detect false information. We recognize clever and flattering falsehoods the instant we encounter them.

4. We meet others who are also searching as well. Perhaps we find a truly valuable group and work there for awhile; perhaps we don't. The group may facilitate our learning, but even a valuable group can take us only so far. Also, we're not asleep to the

politics and undercurrents, even in a valuable group! That's all part of the learning.

5. Even years into this search our love of acquiring knowledge is as robust as ever. We discover the importance of planting these seeds more deeply than reading alone provides. There are several ways, such as collecting pearls in your own *Book of Development*, reading aloud, contemplation and several other tools that bring a whole new level of profit to your study.

6. We're open to ways to spread this knowledge, though it must be passed along to others in appropriate venues and with good manners—never proselytizing. We need not convince anyone of anything. A great relief!

7. A whole new challenge presents itself. We can no longer tolerate such a wide gulf between our actual inner level on one hand, and the fabulous facts now inhabiting our thinking on the other hand. We make a crucial transition. We *apply* the truths we've gathered right in the midst of our daily life. This transition is far more challenging, and potentially far richer, than being in the day-by-day orbit of a great spiritual master. After all, this is where a real teacher is trying to get us to. This step is greatly facilitated by *The Language of Awakening*.

8. Something surprising and unexpected happens. As *applicators* we now encounter increased resistance from the horizontal thinking patterns. Old ways of thinking did not have much of a problem with reading and seminar attendance. But now that we've crossed over to the level of *practice*, it pulls out its bigger guns to threaten and discourage us.

9. At the same time there is increased resistance, there's also amazing moments of cheerfulness. We allow the spirit to infuse our

efforts with its massive capabilities. All kinds of little inner healings happen. This is another major transition. It is necessary at times to press through storms, sometimes severe ones, but when they clear, the Heart is in view.

10. No matter where we are, or who we're around, we enjoy our own company! In earlier years the slightest thing could pull us away. Now the Heart is awake and the vitality pouring out of it is far more interesting than anything the world could give us. This awareness of our Source increases our capacity for good work.

11. The rich vein of gold was, and still is, priceless for our development. Our gratitude is deeper than ever; however, now we suspect that if we cling to the vein of gold we're going to obscure direct revelation of Higher Truths. There are no books and no physical teachers at the outpouring of this Source, and that is where we must dare to go.

12. Silence. There are things the Source has to say, direct to your innermost thoughts, but it cannot and will not say them through a book or through anyone else. The highest spiritual art is that of a quiet Heart that is not churning, but is motionless and listening. The Inner Teacher awakens with your supremely rich and purpose-filled life.

RESOURCES FOR
YOUR JOURNEY

SuperWisdom champions the application of these beautiful truths in the midst of your daily life. You'll learn how to bring a new quality of interest and enjoyment to everything you do.

RESOURCES FOR YOUR JOURNEY

1. **SUPERWISDOM PRESENTS: TIME OUT FOR TRUTH**

   Heard of I-Pods and podcasts? Well, you don't have to have an I-Pod to enjoy this weekly *free* audio broadcast. Your desktop computer works just fine. (But with an MP3 player you can transfer the audio to your mobile listening device.) Find out what it's all about at:

   www.TimeOutForTruth.com

2. **SUPERWISDOM SUBSCRIPTION WEBSITE**

   Visitors can enjoy inspiring free content at the website, but this amazingly affordable subscription opens the doors to a remarkable feast of print, audio and video resources. You also get opportunities to meet friendly men and women all over the world who are studying these ideas. Visit:

www.SuperWisdom.com

3. SUPERWISDOM BOOKSTORES

Visit our Vernon Howard Amazon.com Bookstore and enjoy great discounts on his ten best classics. Also enjoy the Super-Wisdom Bookstore for additional resources.

THE SUPERWISDOM
FOUNDATION

THIS WORK SEEKS the awakening of the Inner Teacher in sincere men and women, thus empowering them to enjoy a life of authentic happiness, independence and harmonious relationships. There is nothing to join at SuperWisdom and we have no creed for you to adopt. The Foundation is an all-volunteer effort and your nonprofit tax deductible support is appreciated. Thank you.

SUPERWISDOM FOUNDATION
P.O. Box 326
Payson, Arizona 85547
PHONE: (773) 353-8696
E-MAIL: *info@SuperWisdom.com*
www.SuperWisdom.com

SUPERWISDOM ELECTRONIC MAGAZINE (FREE EZINE)

The SuperWisdom Ezine inspires thousands of wisdom seekers. There's never paid advertising and your email address is confidential. Subscribe today at www.SuperWisdom.com.